FACING THE POWERS

Thomas H. McAlpine

INNOVATIONS
IN MISSION

Bryant L. Myers, Series Editor

MARC

FACING THE POWERS
What are the options?

Thomas H. McAlpine

Published 1991 by MARC, a division of World Vision International, 919 W. Huntington Drive, Monrovia, California, 91016 USA.

ISBN: 0-912552-72-7

DEDICATION

While this book was still in press, two World Vision colleagues paid the price of confronting the powers with their lives in the streets of Lima. This book is dedicated to them:
José Chuquín
Norm Tattersall

Facing the Powers is the second in MARC's Innovations in Mission series.

Other books in this series:

The Nonresidential Missionary

Empowering the Poor

"Today eighty-five per cent of the world's population lives in poverty to make possible the luxury of the comfortable fifteen per cent. Tomorrow it will be the ninety per cent catering for the luxury of the ten per cent." [Archbishop Helder Camara]. We know this is going on. We know that this way lies Armageddon. Yet successive world trade conferences have failed to change anything of substance. Are we not in the grip of forces beyond ourselves?

—*Michael Green*

Edgardo Silvoso reports the accelerated multiplication of churches within a radius of 100 miles of the city of Rosario (Argentina) after a team broke the power of the spirit of Merigildo in 1985.

—*C. Peter Wagner*

Nationalism is not, one could argue, an unmitigated evil.... But what makes nationalism so pernicious, so death-dealing, so blasphemous, is its seemingly irresistible tendency toward idolatry. In the name of this idol whole generations are maimed, slaughtered, exiled, and made idolaters. One hundred million lives have been offered on the altar of this Moloch thus far in the twentieth century.

—*Walter Wink*

A few weeks earlier smallpox had come to the village and taken a number of children. Doctors trained in Western medicine had tried to halt the plague but without success. Finally, in desperation the village elders had sent for a diviner who told them that Maisamma, Goddess of Smallpox, was angry with the village.

—*Paul Hiebert (India)*

Any version of Christianity is incredible which, while professing belief in the Holy Spirit, fails to carry his power and victory into every deepest hole and corner. What our world needs everywhere today is this exorcism of its demons. For it is only when the heavens open and the Spirit descends that God's good creation comes into being and continues in being.

—*Ernst Käsemann*

CONTENTS

INTRODUCTION

THE 1990s are a time of rapid change in almost every area of life. The political and economic maps are being redrawn. Technology is advancing at a dizzying pace. The center of gravity of Christ's body in the world has shifted to the southern hemisphere. The church is exploding in China and on the Pacific rim. Theology of mission is being written at the grassroots among the poor. The cost of misusing and abusing God's creation is staring us in the face.

In the midst of this climate of rapid change, extreme complexity and almost obsessive pluralism, the church of Jesus Christ is to be in mission. The good news of Jesus Christ and the claims of his kingdom are needed everywhere.

Post-Christian Europe needs to rediscover the gospel that was once central to its culture and sense of being. The nomadic pastoralists—living across the Sahel in Africa, throughout the Middle East, in the eastern provinces of the USSR and in western and southern China— need to hear a gospel "that will fit on the back of a camel." The poor in Latin America need a gospel that restores their relationship with God and reverses the erosion of their quality of life. North Americans need to hear a good news that restores the vibrancy of worship and commitment to social change to their culturally captive brand of Christianity. The rich and powerful everywhere need to hear how difficult it is for them to get in the kingdom of heaven.

MARC is in the business of inspiring vision and motivating mission among those who are taking the whole gospel to the whole world. One of the ways we seek to fulfill our mission is to identify and share the stories of innovations in mission which, in our fallible view, make sense in this kind of changing, chaotic world. We seek to broadcast what we have discovered as good news in mission in hopes that others might find this information useful in enhancing their own mission. This series, *Innovations in Mission*, is the tool we have chosen for sharing this information with the global Christian mission community. We hope it will be valuable to mission strategists and executives, mission professors and students, and all those for whom Christian mission is part of living life with Christ.

Facing the Powers: What Are The Options? is the second book in this series. It addresses one of the most critical issues facing the mission community today: how do we make sense of the principalities and powers? All over the world, folk in mission are beginning to recognize that the biblical language about principalities and powers cannot be dismissed as first-century, pre-scientific superstition. The world of spirits and the supernatural is real and it has an impact on mission.

Sadly, we in the west are ill-equipped to think with clarity and depth because our dominant Enlightenment paradigm has no space for this level of reality. Principalities and powers, witch doctors and shamans, demons and household gods are merely superstition and hence unworthy of critical thinking and scholarly attention. As a result, those brave enough to try to work seriously with these realities are in a sense struggling in the dark. There are few accepted categories, thought forms or conceptual frameworks within which to work. It's a little like trying to build a building without scaffolding or commonly understood symbols on the architect's plans.

Tom McAlpine, MARC's director of urban evangelism, provides a unique survey of mission folk from the various theological traditions who are struggling to make sense of this complex issue. For the first time, readers can see the Reformed, Anabaptist, third wave (spiritual warfare) and social science approaches to this problem laid side by side. It is our hope that folks from each tradition can discover and learn from the thinking of others using a different theological framework. If we can look over each other's shoulders, we may find that each has a part of the truth, and, if we act as a community of faith, together we might move more quickly on our path of faith.

Bryant L. Myers
Series Editor

ONE

Aerial Reconnaissance

IN THE 1930s German Christians began looking for help in understanding the Nazis. Such evil was not supposed to be possible, no more than werewolves or witches' curses or other relics of pre-scientific, pre-enlightenment times. Such evil was more than human. As they looked, they returned to portions of the New Testament:

> For we are not contending against flesh and blood, but against the principalities, against the powers, against the world rulers of this present darkness, against the spiritual hosts of wickedess in the heavenly places (Eph. 6:12).

Hendrikus Berkhof's *Christ and the Powers*, published in 1953, is a classic illustration of this return to infrequently used portions of Scripture. The principalities and powers, Berkhof argued, are the spiritual dimension of the social, cultural, economic and political structures that govern our existence. They are part of God's good creation, but they have rebelled against God. God's reconciling work deals with them—and may include them. Our theology and practice need to take them into account.

The mission challenges in the 1990s are no less formidable than those facing the German Christians in the 1930s. Old and new idolatries abound. Too often the evil we face appears intractable, woven into the structures of our ordinary life. And our culture is searching for more adequate ways of understanding reality as we move toward a post-scientific, post-Enlightenment paradigm. The popularity of "new age" motifs is perhaps the most obvious symptom of this.

Meanwhile, our theologies and missiological strategies need reworking. Whether facing a witch doctor in the bush or a bureaucrat downtown, practitioners and missiologists are coming to agree that we are up against more than flesh and blood. Whether at the World Council of Churches' World Conference on Mission and Evangelism (Melbourne

1980), or the Spiritual Warfare Track at Lausanne II in Manila (July 1989), we Christians are returning to the language of the powers.

That's what this monograph is about: the variety of ways Christians are returning to the language of the powers for the sake of mission.

It is addressed to people in mission and people directing mission. They face mission challenges for which traditional theologies or strategies are inadequate. There are a variety of options being offered for dealing with the principalities and powers. While Kellermann and Peretti both talk about the powers, they aren't proposing the same model for mission. We hope this monograph will help people better to evaluate the options.

We will be focusing on the interaction of the principalities and powers with entire human communities or cultures. We will not address issues of demonic influence or possession of individuals. These tend to be issues in pastoral care, rather than in mission. Nevertheless, this distinction blurs in some interesting ways, and we will try to attend to this.

The Traditions

We Christians are returning to the language of the powers, but in such different ways that we are often talking past each other. We speak from within particular traditions, with all their attendant strengths and weaknesses. We need to hear each other more clearly, learn better from each other, so that we may do mission better—maybe even in closer cooperation. That too is the agenda for this monograph.

What are these differing traditions within which we speak? We will look at four: Reformed, Anabaptist, third wave, and social science. The first three are used as classic types; the last overlaps the first three.

> *The Reformed tradition* emphasizes transforming the power mediated by social structures toward greater compatibility with the gospel.

> *The Anabaptist tradition* emphasizes the freedom given by the gospel over against the power mediated by social structures.

> *The third wave tradition* emphasizes miraculous divine power in contrast to the power mediated by social structures.

> *The social science tradition* attempts to relate the biblical language about the powers to models of reality developed using the social sciences.

"Reformed" and "Anabaptist" are used as a short-hand for the contrast between understanding the gospel as transforming the powers, and understanding the gospel as an alternative to the powers. While the contrast reflects historic divisions within Protestantism, it is used more broadly here. As we will use it here, it cuts across the Protestant/Catholic divide. Some Catholics are covered with the Anabaptists, and most liberation theologians would fall in the Reformed group.

The language of the principalities and powers has a healthy life within the Reformed tradition, where its mission implications continue to be explored. Hendrikus Berkhof's formulation remains central. Michael Green takes it up in his *I Believe in Satan's Downfall*. Robert Linthicum develops it to make sense of what urban pastors and community organizers face daily. Walter Wink draws on it as well, responding to challenges of ministry in Latin America and South Africa. Bill Kellermann draws on Wink for ministry in Detroit. This is hardly an exhaustive list. Oscar Cullmann, Stephen Charles Mott or Richard Mouw are equally deserving of inclusion.

On the Anabaptist side, Gerhard Lohfink's *Jesus and Community* provides a powerful contemporary statement of the Anabaptist vision for the church. Norbert Lohfink's *Option for the Poor* fleshes out that same vision, drawing on the Old Testament. John Howard Yoder—Berkhof's translator—has incorporated Berkhof's language into his model of discipleship. Vernard Eller continues this tradition. Others, including the Blumhardts, Jacques Ellul or René Padilla, could also have been included.

While "Reformed" and "Anabaptist" are familiar categories, "third wave" needs more explanation. The name was coined by C. Peter Wagner. It recognizes three major movements of the Holy Spirit in this century: the classic pentecostal movement at the beginning of the century, the charismatic renewal movement of the '60s and '70s, and the evangelical discovery of spiritual gifts in the '80s. The "third wave" affirms its links with the previous waves, but distinguishes itself from them in that it does not promote a single "baptism in the Spirit" and does not give special status to the gift of tongues. For this reason, the third wave group does not describe itself as "charismatic" or "pentecostal." We will use the term "third wave" for this group, while leaving open the question of the involvement of those from previous waves.

A major concern within the third wave tradition is how to evangelize geographical areas that appear to be strangely resistant to the gospel. This tradition characteristically views the powers as opposing evangelism, and often uses a kind of territorial exorcism to deal with them. Their perspective had a high profile in the sessions on spiritual warfare at Lausanne II in Manila, and it was later reflected in a consultation on the subject of territorial spirits. Wagner has collected many stories on this subject, and is working on an interpretive framework. Tom White heads a deliverance ministry in Oregon. John Dawson is the Southwest U.S. Director of Youth with a Mission, and has recently published *Taking our*

Cities for God: How to Break Spiritual Strongholds. Frank Peretti's novels both exemplify and nurture this tradition.

The social science tradition is a different sort of grouping. Most of those surveyed within this group could as well be placed elsewhere (Shuster with the Reformed, Hiebert with the Anabaptist, etc). What holds this grouping together is their attempt to relate the biblical language about principalities and powers to models of reality developed by the social sciences. On the strength of this common goal we refer to it also as a tradition.

From the psychological side, a number of people draw on Carl Jung. Morton Kelsey is one example. Also working on the psychology/theology border, but outside the Jungian paradigm, is Marguerite Shuster. From the anthropological side, Paul Hiebert provides an example.

The writers and practitioners which we will be surveying are both working the same and different problems. They are working the same problem in that they are responding to the collapse of the old Enlightenment, modernist, and scientific paradigms. They are trying to find something more adequate to make sense of the supernatural or spiritual dimensions of our world. They are working different problems, however, in that they are working within specific traditions which highlight in characteristic ways the contours of sin and salvation, brokenness and healing.

Finally, a word on the use of "rediscovering" in the monograph's subtitle. We are all attempting to move beyond the Enlightenment paradigms which neatly divided the world into secular and sacred, public and private, natural and supernatural. The way forward, however, is not clear. A return to a pre-Enlightenment or pre-scientific position is not really an option. Perhaps comparing the way different traditions are struggling with these issues will help the pioneering process of rediscovery.

The Words

The focus in our survey is on implications for the church in mission. One necessary test of the adequacy of any mission thinking is its compatibility with Scripture. To help the reader keep the biblical material easily in view, here are some key texts that play a role in the discussion (RSV):

> When the Most High gave to the nations their inheritance, when he separated the sons of men, he fixed the bounds of the peoples according to the number of the sons of God. For the LORD's portion is his people, Jacob his allotted heritage *Deut. 32:8-9.*

God has taken his place in the divine council; in the midst of the gods he holds judgment: "How long will you judge unjustly and show partiality to the wicked? [Selah] Give justice to the weak and the fatherless; maintain the right of the afflicted and the destitute. Rescue the weak and the needy; deliver them from the hand of the wicked" *Ps. 82:1-4* .

The prince of the kingdom of Persia withstood me twenty-one days; but Michael, one of the chief princes, came to help me, so I left him there with the prince of the kingdom of Persia and came to make you understand what is to befall your people in the latter days. For the vision is for days yet to come *Dan. 10:13-14.*

Or how can one enter a strong man's house and plunder his goods, unless he first binds the strong man? Then indeed he may plunder his house *Matt. 12:29.*

Immediately after the tribulation of those days the sun will be darkened, and the moon will not give its light, and the stars will fall from heaven, and the powers *(dunamis)* of the heavens will be shaken *Matt. 24:29.*

And when they bring you before the synagogues and the rulers *(arche)* and the authorities *(exousia)*, do not be anxious how or what you are to answer or what you are to say *Luke 12:11.*

For I am sure that neither death, nor life, nor angels, nor principalities *(archon)* nor things present, nor things to come, nor powers *(dunamis)*, nor height, nor depth, nor anything else in all creation, will be able to separate us from the love of God in Christ Jesus our Lord *Rom. 8:38-39.*

Let every person be subject to the governing authorities *(exousia)*. For there is no authority except from God, and those that exist have been instituted by God. Therefore he who resists the authorities resists what God has appointed, and those who resist will incur judgment *Rom. 13:1-2a.*

Yet among the mature we do impart wisdom, although it is not a wisdom of this age or of the rulers *(archon)* of this age, who are doomed to pass away. But we impart a secret and hidden wisdom of God, which God decreed before the ages for our glorification. None of the rulers *(archon)* of this age understood this; for if they had, they would not have crucified the Lord of glory *1 Cor. 2:6-8.*

Then comes the end, when he delivers the kingdom to God the Father after destroying every rule *(arche)* and every authority *(exousia)* and power *(dunamis)*. For he must reign until he has put all his enemies under his feet. The last enemy to be destroyed is death *1 Cor. 15:24-26.*

For though we live in the world we are not carrying on a worldly war, for the weapons of our warfare are not worldly but have divine power to destroy strongholds *2 Cor. 10:3-4.*

... which he accomplished in Christ when he raised him from the dead and made him sit at his right hand in the heavenly places, far above all rule *(arche)* and authority *(exousia)* and power *(dunamis)* and dominion *(kuriotes)*, and above every name that is named, not only in this age but also in that which is to come *Eph.1:20-21.*

And you he made alive, when you were dead through the trespasses and sins in which you once walked, following the course of this world, following the prince *(archon)* of the power of the air, the spirit that is now at work in the sons of disobedience *Eph. 2:1-2.*

... that through the church the manifold wisdom of God might now be made known to the principalities *(archon)* and powers *(exousia)* in the heavenly places *Eph. 3:10.*

For we are not contending against flesh and blood, but against the principalities *(archon)*, against the powers *(exousia)*, against the world rulers *(kosmokrator)* of this present darkness, against the spiritual hosts of wickedness in the heavenly places *Eph. 6:12.*

... for in him all things were created, in heaven and on earth, visible and invisible, whether thrones *(thronos)* or dominions *(kuriotes)* or principalities *(archon)* or authorities *(exousia)*—all things were created through him and for him. He is before all things, and in him all things hold together. He is the head of the body, the church; he is the beginning, the first-born from the dead, that in everything he might be pre-eminent. For in him all the fulness of God was pleased to dwell, and through him to reconcile to himself all things, whether on earth or in heaven, making peace by the blood of his Cross *Col. 1:16-20.*

... and you have come to fullness of life in him, who is the head of all rule *(arche)* and authority *(exousia) Col. 2:10.*

He disarmed the principalities *(archon)* and powers *(exousia)* and made a public example of them, triumphing over them in him *Col. 2:15.*

Remind them to be submissive to rulers *(arche)* and authorities *(exousia)*, to be obedient, to be ready for any honest work *Titus 3:1.*

... who has gone into heaven and is at the right hand of God, with angels, authorities *(exousia)*, and powers *(dunamis)* subject to him *1 Pet. 3:22.*

TWO

Transformation by Osmosis:
The Reformed Tradition

BY THE START of this century, the liberal Protestant theologies had almost swept away Europe's ghosts, ghoulies, and nightmares. Conservatives complained that liberal Christianity was bloodless, but the complaint had little force as long as bloodless Christianity seemed to work. Then came one war, and then another, with Hitler and his neo-pagan parades, icons, myths, and human sacrifices. Before it was over, six million Jews were dead, two atomic bombs had been dropped, and human extinction was a daily threat.

How does one do mission in such a context, particularly since mission intersects with the state at so many points? Simple appeals to Romans 13 or Revelation 13 are clearly not enough. What might be the truly Christian course? Hendrikus Berkhof's *Christ and the Powers* attempts to answer that question.

Hendrikus Berkhof

Berkhof studies Paul's references to the powers: Rom. 8:38f; 1 Cor. 2:8; 15:24-26; Eph. 1:20f; 2:1f; 3:10; 6:12; Col. 1:16; 2:15. Paul did not invent the principalities and powers, for apocalyptic and rabbinic literature often refers to them. In this literature the powers are personal, spiritual beings who act on earth, especially within nature. The powers are a separate subject apart from their dealings with humanity. Where they affect humanity, it is usually in nature—or politics.

Paul, however, talks about the principalities and powers differently. He is not concerned with the powers apart from their role in the human drama. But he explores their role in the human drama in multiple spheres.

In fact, Berkhof argues that Paul has "demythologized" the powers. They are less heavenly angels and more structures of earthly existence. So while many take the principalities and powers to be angels, Berkhof dissents. If they are good angels, it's hard to explain the texts that picture them as opponents. If they're bad angels, it's equally hard to explain their involvement in creation, preservation and reconciliation. The powers are "a category of their own" (1962, 19). It is not even clear whether the powers are personal beings or personifications. In any case, Berkhof regards this as a minor point.

The powers play a paradoxical role. Col. 1:15-17 speaks of the powers as part of creation, and, as such, presumably good. When we look at traditions, morality, institutions of family, city or state, we are looking at the principalities and powers. Life without these would be nasty, brutish, and short. However, after the fall, the powers also separate us from God. For example, respect for the ancestors in China or Shintoism in Japan preserve life, but also often block people from seeing God's revelation in Jesus. We misunderstand the principalities and powers when we downplay either their preserving or obstructing role. And, when we misunderstand the powers, it is more difficult to respond appropriately to them.

But the Cross, according to Paul, undoes the powers (Col. 2:13-15). This is not an obvious claim. Rome crucified thousands in Judaea in the first century, and was not noticeably weaker. So how does Jesus' Cross disarm the powers? The weapon the powers wield, Berkhof argues, is not physical but ideological: the claim to legitimacy and power. When this claim is decisively rejected, the inadequacy of physical power is unmasked, as recent events in the Philippines and Eastern Europe show. This is how God defeated the powers at the Cross. The self-proclaimed guardians of truth and justice were caught crucifying God. After the Cross, no claim by the powers to Justice, Truth, or Ultimacy can be heard with a straight face.

Is God going to destroy the principalities and powers? Some translations of 1 Cor. 15:24 suggest this: "Then comes the end, when he delivers the kingdom to God the Father after destroying every rule and every authority and power." But "after dethroning every rule and every authority and power" is also a possible translation, and, Berkhof argues, supported by Col. 1:19. "God reconciles the Powers—and not only men— with Himself through Christ's death" (1962, 33).

What does this mean for us? Berkhof suggests:

1. The church, as a community characterized by freedom and reconciliation, is itself a sign to the powers;
2. "Positive" or "aggressive" approaches to the powers are superfluous; and

3. Attempts to engage the powers directly when the church is not characterized by freedom and reconciliation will be "unfruitful" at best.

As Christ throws the principalities and powers into crisis, what are the possible results? Secularization, nihilism, and restoration are possible, but so is Christianization. As Berkhof puts it, "the Powers, instead of being ideological centers, are what God meant them to be: helps, instruments, giving shape and direction to the genuine life of man as child of God and as neighbor" (1962, 49).

We can summarize Berkhof's vision with the statements and accompanying figures on the next page.

Michael Green

Michael Green's *I Believe in Satan's Downfall* has a clear missions slant. On the one hand, Satan's downfall is good news to the beleaguered. On the other hand, it serves as a warning, for the fall of Satan means the fall of Satan's subsidiaries. It's worth double-checking where one's investments are.

Green devotes a chapter to the principalities and powers. Much of Green's treatment parallels Berkhof's. At other points he diverges, first regarding the nature of the powers, and second in providing examples of their current work.

Regarding the nature of the powers, Green cites Heinrich Schlier, a New Testament scholar, to argue that the demons in the Gospels and the principalities and powers in Paul shouldn't be separated (1981, 82). This is a key point, for it affects how we see the powers' present and future. Further, while this point is often asserted, evidence is seldom presented. What is Schlier's evidence?

> In my opinion they are always wicked powers, that is, hostile to God and to Christ. This is true even of Eph. 1:21; 3:10; Col. 1:16; 2:10, for there is no reason for distinguishing the *archai kai exousiai* of these texts from those which are mentioned in Rom. 8:38; 1 Cor. 15:24; Eph. 6:12 and Col. 2:15; and in the latter texts they are certainly hostile powers (1961, 14n13).

Here Schlier is simply using one group of texts to neutralize another group. We are no closer to understanding the early chapters of Ephesians and Colossians. We are certainly no closer to interacting with Berkhof's more nuanced reading. In sum, while Schlier may be correct, he has not given us enough evidence to convince. The point is worth stressing since Wagner reprints Green's chapter in his *Territorial Spirits Reader* (1990).

A visualization of Hendrikus Berkhof's view

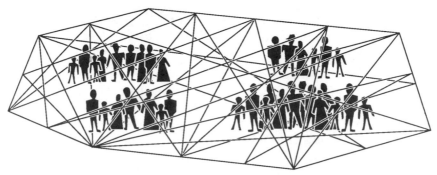

HUMAN EXISTENCE is captive to structures that both preserve and destroy life. We are both sinners and sinned-against.

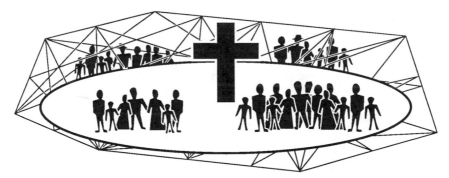

GOD'S SALVATION reconciles us to God and our neighbor, freeing us from these structures by placing us in the church. (It is in this context that we can make some sense of the claim "Outside the church there is no salvation.")

GOD HAS NOT written off the powers; the church is tied—somehow—to their redemption.

Where are these powers at work? Green considers both the world and the church. In the world, our consumer society perverts values, and impoverishes the many for the sake of the few. Consider coffee, or infant formula. Coffee is one of El Salvador's major exports, but the deck is stacked: "a tractor which cost 165 bags of coffee in 1960 cost 316 ten years later" (1981, 101). Multi-nationals sell infant formula in poor countries where living conditions make it almost impossible to use it properly. Green asserts "the graveyards of the Third World bear silent testimony to the grip the principalities and powers exercise upon something as basic as baby foods" (1981, 102). Other examples include state torture, the arms race, the loss of moral absolutes, environmental degradation, and devalued sexuality.

In the church, Green points to secularism, denominationalism, loss of vision, officialdom, dependence on the world for moral guidance, and a consumer lifestyle. Regarding the latter, Green sees John Taylor's, Ronald Sider's, and Michael Harper's fight for a simple lifestyle to be a fight against the powers.

So what is the Christian response to the powers? Watchfulness, prayer, boldness, resistance, and involvement. Green cites Bonhoeffer, Archbishop Helder Camara, Martin Luther King Jr., and the French resistance during World War II as examples.

Robert Linthicum

Robert Linthicum heads World Vision's Office of Urban Advance, which supports World Vision field offices by developing urban mission strategies for the mega-cities of the two-thirds world. Linthicum embraced the language of the principalities and powers as he sought to understand and meet the massive challenges facing him as an urban minister. His *City of God, City of Satan* (1991) picks up the Reformed themes and applies them to the city. While his language reflects his debt to Wink, he sees the powers as personal spiritual beings.

> The political system of a city is infused with a spiritual essence, a "soul," unimagined and unexplored inner depths. The angel of a city is the inner spirituality that broods over that city. And that spirituality has immense power—either for good or for ill.
>
> What is it that you feel in a Calcutta, a Moscow, a Bangkok, a Mexico City, a Washington, a Nairobi? I would suggest that what you sense is the soul of that city. The angel of each city infuses and dominates the principali-

ties and powers, systems and structures, people groups and individuals of that city.

In the urban workshops I lead around the world, I ask those in attendance to identify the angel of their city. They determine together who the angel of their city is, name and describe him, and then consider how that angel manifests himself in their city's structures, systems and people, and, finally, in their own churches. . . . to be able to name your city's angel and to understand how he is at work both exposes him and enables you to understand the dimensions the church's ministry must undertake if it is truly to confront the principalities and powers (1990, 115-17)!

What does this mean in practice? Linthicum shared some stories during an interview.

The Corn Exchange Building in the heart of Chicago's financial district is topped by the goddess of wheat. That says a great deal about Chicago, crowned by an absolute commitment to "turning a buck." It was tremendously helpful to see this, that the essential struggle in ministry was an economic struggle. In one neighborhood the battle was between the people and the economic movers and shakers of Chicago who wanted to take it over. They wanted to redline it so that property values would plummet, buy it up, raze it, and build high-rise condos. We saw as we organized around this issue that we had to make it in the self-interest of the banks and insurance companies to change their strategies.

In an urban ministry workshop in Bangkok, participants found prostitution a particularly apt symbol for making sense of their city. Bangkok was a beautiful young maiden, and remained so while the Kingdom of Siam stayed unspotted. But she has been raped by the economic powers of the first world—and was not an entirely unwilling victim. Examples include Bangkok's tourist-driven prostitution, and loss of cultural integrity. A hundred years ago, Bangkok was a sensual city, beautiful. Now she is simply sexual. What does this mean for ministry? Conversation turned to the churches of Bangkok, in which the fastest growing are those which imitate the West. An occasion for praise, or another example of prostitution?

Further, Linthicum's model of action and reflection in community organizing highlights the role of the powers. Notice the path reflection takes in the diagram on the next page! Once one gets to the real issues, attempts to address them reveal the principalities and powers. Attempts to address these lead to recognition of the group's own complicity in these systems. The problem is not simply out there. At that point, if the group does not go into denial or legalism or some other dodge, the gospel's news of forgiveness takes on profound significance. Awareness of the powers means both more profound confession, and a search for spiritual disciplines which can sustain one in the conflict.

Notice, too, that the principalities and powers are not the first topic of action or reflection. The model strongly implies that if there are times when one should be talking about the powers, there are also times when one should not be talking about the powers.

Linthicum's work is of interest, then, for two reasons. First, he is seeking to use the language of the principalities and powers for analysis in urban situations in both the first and two-thirds worlds. Second, he is developing a ministry model in which knowledge of and engagement with the powers plays an important role.

Walter Wink

Walter Wink, professor of Biblical Interpretation at Auburn Theological Seminary, spent four months in Latin America in 1982. His perceptions of the many abuses of power there forced him to rethink his theology and missiology of power. He is two thirds of the way through his trilogy on the powers: *Naming the Powers: The Language of Power in the New Testament* (1984) and *Unmasking the Powers: The Invisible Forces that Determine Human Existence* (1986). The third projected volume, *Engaging the Powers*, is not yet in press. This partly reflects the challenge of the topic, and partly reflects the pressures of his work in South Africa.

As this trilogy represents the most sustained treatment of our theme, we treat Wink in more detail. Wink interprets the powers as impersonal and bipolar:

> ... the "principalities and powers" are the inner and outer aspects of any given manifestation of power. As the inner aspect they are the spirituality of institutions, the "within" of corporate structures and systems, the inner essence of outer organizations of power. As the outer aspect they are political systems, appointed officials, the

The Reflection/Action Cycle in Community Organizing

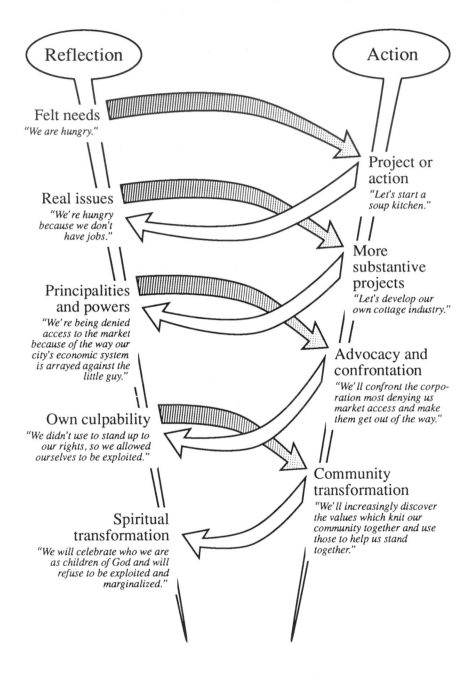

Reflection

Action

Felt needs
"We are hungry."

Project or action
"Let's start a soup kitchen."

Real issues
"We're hungry because we don't have jobs."

More substantive projects
"Let's develop our own cottage industry."

Principalities and powers
"We're being denied access to the market because of the way our city's economic system is arrayed against the little guy."

Advocacy and confrontation
"We'll confront the corporation most denying us market access and make them get out of the way."

Own culpability
"We didn't use to stand up to our rights, so we allowed ourselves to be exploited."

Community transformation
"We'll increasingly discover the values which knit our community together and use those to help us stand together."

Spiritual transformation
"We will celebrate who we are as children of God and will refuse to be exploited and marginalized."

"chair" of an organization, laws—in short, all the tangible manifestations which power takes. Every Power tends to have a visible pole, an outer form—be it a church, a nation, or an economy—and an invisible pole, an inner spirit or driving force that animates, legitimates, and regulates its physical manifestation in the world. Neither pole is the cause of the other. Both come into existence together and cease to exist together (1984, 5).

What is Wink's evidence? Wink pulls together exegetical, psychological, and philosophical arguments. From the exegetical side, Wink notes that the New Testament has a rich vocabulary for power, and is consistently concerned with questions of power. But previous studies on power have erred by importing our sharp distinction between spiritual and non-spiritual into the texts. So it is a dubious method to separate out the spiritual powers as a separate topic. For instance, "in a single chapter, only six verses apart, Luke uses *exousia* in reference to the 'power' of Satan (12:5) and to human 'authorities' (12:11)" (1984, 9). And Colossians 1:16 appears to establish this bipolar nature of the powers (outer and inner aspects):

For in him [the Son] all things were created, in heaven and on earth, visible and invisible, whether thrones (*thronoi*) or dominions (*kyriotetes*) or principalities (*archai*) or authorities (*exousiai*)—all things were created through him and for him (1984, 11).

From the psychological side, Wink appeals to Jung, arguing that Jung's archetypes correspond to the inner aspect or pole of the powers. Thus the Bible and psychology dovetail. From the philosophical side, Wink appeals to Whitehead, whose system offers a way of teasing out the meaning of the "inner" and "outer" aspects of manifestations of power. It is not that Wink is arguing for one psychological or philosophical tradition over another. Rather, Wink appears to be using Jung and Whitehead as helps for those who find traditional explanations of human existence to be unpalatable, and is not himself interested in advancing a particular ontological position. For that reason, we have dealt with Wink here among the Reformed—justified by his cheerful advocacy of political power—rather than in the social science tradition.

If Wink is not focusing on the ontological question, what questions is he focusing on? The answer is mission and ministry strategies. For example, treating Ephesians 6, Wink argues that we are not just dealing with defensive strategies against the principalities and powers:

> The terms employed are taken straight from the legionnaire's equipment, and the metaphor is of the church like the Roman wedge, the most efficient and terrifying military formation known up to that time and for some thousand years after. . . . when the lines closed the legionnaire used the short two-edged *gladius* (Gk., *machaira*) to thrust up under the enemy's shield and disembowel him. In such close quarters the long swords used by most of Rome's enemies were rendered ineffective (1984, 86).

Paul "depicts the church taking the fight to the enemy, and *he expects the church to win*" (1984, 88).

Eph. 3:10 offers a different picture, largely a riddle. How does the church make known God's wisdom to the principalities and powers? We will probably have to wait for Wink's third volume for a full treatment. He drops some interesting hints. The structure of power means that evangelism is social action (if done properly)—and vice versa. In some situations "Jesus is Lord" draws yawns, but "Jesus, friend of the poor" draws bullets, so "fidelity to the gospel lies not in repeating its slogans but in plunging the prevailing idolatries into its corrosive acids" (1984, 111). "We are to work with determined persistence at the outer, and to trust God to change the inner" (1984, 127).

Wink's second volume, *Unmasking the Powers*, takes up Satan, demons, gods, the elements of the universe, and the angels of churches, nations, and nature. Wink's treatment of demons and the angels of nations are relevant here.

Regarding demons, the demonic today is often explained either as an effect of social pathology (the approach of Marxists, liberation theologians, etc.) or as an effect of personal developmental malfunctions (the viewpoint of the psychological mainstream). This, suggests Wink, is an inadequate, even unneeded, choice.

Wink suggests "there are three types of demonic manifestations: outer personal possession, collective possession, and the inner personal demonic" (1986, 43). Outer personal possession, as exemplified by the story of the Gerasene demoniac, is "merely the personal pole of a collective malady afflicting an entire society" (1986, 50). Exorcism — with multiple safeguards—is indicated. Nevertheless, to stop with exorcism is to deal only with symptoms.

Regarding collective possession, Wink reminds us that for the early church, baptism was also an exorcism: "It regarded *everyone* prior to baptism as possessed, by virtue of nothing more than belonging to a world in rebellion against God" (1986, 51). Collective possession has been invoked to explain Nazi Germany; it is relevant to us today. Jesus' cleansing of the temple may be an example of exorcism directed towards collective possession. Social protest cast as exorcism will enable us to take the evil facing us more seriously:

> Symbolic acts of social protest gain a dimension of depth by being formulated as explicit rites of exorcism. One of the drawbacks of any act of protest is that the very specificity of the demand for change implies that a suitable response to the demand would satisfy the protesters. The ritual act of exorcism, on the other hand, unveils an entire system of death behind the specific wrong. It saves us from reformist naiveté and superficial utopianism by revealing the link between the immediate injustice and the entire network of injustices that the kingdom of death maintains at the willing behest of those who benefit from evil (1986, 67).

Finally, with regard to the inner personal demonic, Jesus' teaching (Mark 7:14-15, 21-23) suggests that we deal with "inner demons" not through exorcism (in sharp contrast to the third wave tradition) but by reintegrating them into our persons. On this point Wink's approach is parallel to Kelsey's (discussed below).

Regarding the angels of the nations, texts such as Deut. 32:8-9 and Daniel 10 suggest that angels are also associated with nations. Perhaps, with Origen, the "man of Macedonia" (Acts 16:9) was the angel of Macedonia. As Wink summarizes his argument,

> The gods or angels of the nations have a discernible personality and vocation . . . are a part of the redemptive plan of God . . . our role in this redemptive activity is to acknowledge their existence, love them as creatures of God, unmask their idolatries, and stir up in them their heavenly vocation (1986, 88).

We have some sense what the personality of a nation might be about, since we are familiar with national distinctives. But vocation? The precondition to discovering vocation is repentance, repentance of selfish pursuit of the nation's own interests. (And *that* precondition is daunting enough so that Wink does not push the question of discovering vocation further.) Nevertheless, the nations will be redeemed (Rev. 15:4; 21:26).

This model, Wink suggests, will enable us better to unmask the idolatries of nations. This unmasking must be done in love. The protesters against the war in Vietnam misstepped badly in talking about "Amerikkka," "People do not change national attitudes and policies simply because they are told they are wrong. They change because of love for their country" (1986, 104).

After all this, what might the angel of the U.S. say? Wink offers an answer, which includes:

> My light of hope is still raised over your shore, and more people than ever in history are fleeing to me, yet my hands are tied by the dark power created by your worship of things. Wealth is your real god, and all your gravest sins have been committed for it. You bought and sold slaves and killed my native peoples for wealth, you intervene in foreign lands for wealth, you sacrifice your own children in wars fought for control of world markets, and you demonize Communists because they challenge your system of wealth. . . . I need help. I cannot get through to my own people. They listen only to their idols. You must come to my aid, even as I have come to yours, now that you have become open to me (1986, 107).

The missiological bottom line of this second volume? Wink argued previously "when a particular Power becomes idolatrous . . . then that Power becomes demonic. The church's task is to unmask this idolatry and recall the Powers to their created purposes in the world" (1984, 5). In this volume Wink has explored some of the ways in which the powers become idolatrous, wreaking havoc in both our individual lives and in the lives of our communities. We need to become familiar with how the powers can go bad, so that we will be able to recognize it and—God help us— deal with it.

Christians in South Africa invited Wink to give seminars on nonviolence in the spring of 1986; *Violence and Nonviolence in South Africa: Jesus' Third Way* was the result. Its thesis is that Jesus' third way, love of enemies or creative nonviolence, must also be our way. Can this be anything other than the central statement on the topic of engaging the powers (the projected third volume in Wink's trilogy)? So, what does Wink suggest?

Fight and flight are the two ways our biology prepares us to deal with evil. Jesus offers the third way: militant nonviolence. Wink develops this point starting with the text that appears to work against it: Matt. 5:39 ("Do not resist an evildoer"). This has always been a puzzling text in light of Jesus' actions; Wink suggests that 'resist' badly translates *antistenai* (cf Mark 15:7 or Acts 19:40) and that a better translation would be "Do not strike back at evil (or, one who has done you evil) in kind. Do not give blow for blow. Do not retaliate against violence with violence" (1987, 13). Wink turns to the examples which follow (Matt. 5:39-41), arguing that they support this reading. For example, if you are being sued by a creditor for your outer garment, give him your inner one as well. Which leaves you naked.

> There stands the creditor, beet-red with embarrassment, your outer garment in the one hand, your underwear in the other. You have suddenly turned the tables on him. You had no hope of winning the trial; the law was entirely in his favor. But you have refused to be humiliated, and at the same time you have registered a stunning protest against a system that spawns such debt. . . . . The creditor is revealed to be not a "respectable" money-lender but a party in the reduction of an entire social class to landlessness and destitution. This unmasking is not simply punitive, however; it offers the creditor a chance to see, perhaps for the first time in his life, what his practices cause, and to repent (1987, 18-19).

Not surprisingly, Wink's examples of this response include Martin Luther King, the Danes during World War II, and Saul Alinsky.

> Nonviolent militant action is crucial in the encounter with principalities and powers, for they are never simply the outer forms of institutions, structures and systems, but also comprise the interiority or withinness of these outer forms—their spirituality (1987, viii).

The problem with violence is that it does not cut deep enough: "It is not the advocates but the very spirit of apartheid itself that must be killed" (1987, 40).

Why nonviolence? Wink's reasons clarify the nature of the spiritual warfare he sees us all involved in.

1. The love of enemies. The Rev. James Bevel, a protagonist in the U.S. civil rights movement, gave an impromptu speech which included these lines: "It's not enough to defeat [Sheriff] Jim Clark—do you hear me Jim?—we want you converted. We cannot win by hating our oppressors. We have to love them into changing." Again, "[Martin Luther] King [Jr.] enabled his followers to see the white racist also as a victim of the Principalities and Powers" (1987, 53-54).

2. The means are commensurate with the new order. "Violence simply is not radical enough, since it generally changes only the actors but not the way power is exercised" (1987,

58). How power is used may be as important as who is exercising it. To "defeat" the powers while using power their way may be a contradiction in terms.

3. Respect for the rule of law. "The Biblical understanding of the Powers is that they are indeed fallen but not totally depraved. Even when they are repressive in the extreme, they still embody something that must be honored and to which we must subject ourselves: the *principle of law*" (1987, 61).

4. Rooting out the violence within. "It is hard enough getting people to engage in Jesus' way of resistance to evil. Then we tell them they have to go through an arduous spiritual discipline to neutralize the oppressor within! As Shelley Douglass puts it, we do not want to have to change our lives to bring about justice. The hardest moment comes when our own internal oppressor meets the outside reality that it supports. It is not out there, but in me, that the oppressor must die" (1987, 65).

5. Not a law but a gift. There is no room for judging here, e.g., judging those who use violence. But this does not mean downplaying the value of the gift of nonviolence. Wink cites Miguel D'Escoto, a priest and former Sandinista official:

> To be very frank with you, I don't think that violence is Christian. . . . I have come to believe that creative nonviolence has to be a constitutive element of evangelization and of the proclamation of the gospel. But in Nicaragua nonviolence was never included in the process of evangelization (1987, 67-68).

This is a loss when nonviolence is needed as a response. But Wink's discussion also implies that evangelization is impoverished if the social meaning of the Cross—including nonviolence—is not made clear.

6. The way of the Cross. Nonviolence is Jesus' chosen way of dealing with evil.

> The Cross also means not necessarily winning. The Principalities and Powers are so colossal, entrenched and determined that the odds for their overthrow or repentance are minuscule, whatever means we use. It is precisely because

the outcome is in question, however, that we
need to choose a way of living that already is a
living of the outcome we desire (1987, 69-70).

One confronts the powers by loving those in bondage to the powers
with a love which is confrontive, creative, uppity, and cruciform. This
love cheerfully wields whatever political power may be available. Wink
will doubtless round out this picture in his third volume, for he has
already also pointed us to weapons like evangelism and exorcism. But
love looks to be the core.

Bill Kellermann

Bill Kellermann, a pastor and professor in Detroit, has drawn on
Wink as a resource for ministry in Detroit. He has shared this both in
articles in *Sojourners*, and in a series of Bible studies for the recent SCUPE
Congress on Urban Ministry. Out of his work in Detroit he has suggested
a generic process (described in Appendix 3) for discerning the spirit of a
city.

In 1988 a move to legalize casino gambling was defeated at the
polls. Why? One citizen said "'I don't know, I'm not sure how to say this.
Detroit is a blue-collar town. Its essential character is just a bad fit for
casinos, with their big money and glitz. From an image perspective it just
doesn't work." "What," Kellermann asks, "if the city of Detroit, its spirit
and identity, was an ally . . . in the fight against the casino invasion?"
(1989, 16).

In fact, "The Spirit of Detroit" is the name of a large sculpture in
downtown Detroit. It shows up on the city's letterhead and is often the
site for demonstrations. Kellermann describes one of these:

> Most intriguing is a weekly vigil of the Anti-Handgun
> Association. At the foot of the sculpture they read aloud
> a small booklet of facts and the stories of victims. It is a
> kind of meditation, a liturgy really. Included is a modi-
> fied verse of the black spiritual, "Were you there when
> each day a child was shot?" But the refrain at the close of
> each small section is "Spirit of Detroit, save our youth!"
> I believe the angel of Detroit is being named and ad-
> dressed in this little event (1989, 19).

A group of Christians began meeting to explore what seeing the city in
this way might mean for mission. And much of Kellermann's article
reflects the activity of this group. It became clear, for instance, that to
speak of the angel of Detroit is not necessarily to speak of power:

At one session of our "Discerning the Angel" group, we tried to bring our own unconscious resources, our right brains, as it is said, into the process by forming an image of Detroit's angel in clay. I found myself shaping up a figure crying out in the grip of a gigantic hand.

Was that hand the power of the multinational auto companies? I think perhaps it was. Though it might in equal portion have been the grip of the cocaine powers (1989, 20).

Regarding the latter point, Kellermann notes that groups of citizens, often supported by the church, have started parading through communities, singing "We shall overcome" in front of houses where drugs are sold. "This is an exorcism, dear friends" (1989, 20).

Kellermann provides an appropriate stopping point for our survey with his witness to groups of Christians attempting to minister in a very difficult situation, and finding in the Bible's references to the powers a resource for that ministry. For this is what all—in whatever tradition—are searching for: not more theories, but resources for ministry in which the alternative to ministry is despair.

Summary

There is significant agreement and disagreement within the Reformed tradition. We will summarize this tradition by using a framework of ten basic questions. They are not the only set of questions we could ask, but they're a place to start. We'll use these questions later to profile the other traditions. As for the answers, while we are primarily summarizing Berkhof, Green, Linthicum, Wink and Kellermann, on occasion we refer to other writers or reports (listed in our bibliography).

1. To what texts does this tradition characteristically appeal?	Col. 1:13-15 (the powers part of an originally good creation, and woven into human institutions); Col. 1:19 (God reconciling all things, including, presumably, the powers).
2. Are the powers personal spiritual beings?	Berkhof thinks Paul leaves the question open, and so leaves it open himself. Some, like Green, see the powers as personal spiritual beings. Wink suggests that the

powers have both an inner spiritual and outer institutional aspect. Mouw's question is still relevant: "Did Paul really think that in speaking of Powers he was referring to distinct entities which operated as causal factors with respect to human affairs? And if he did, are *we* required to posit the existence of such entities?" (1976, 95). We need, he suggests, "an 'ontology' of the Powers" (1976, 95).

3. Are the powers integrally connected to cultures, societies, etc?

Yes. It would be hard to conceive of cultures and societies apart from the powers. This view holds that the powers sustain, as opposed to "infect," institutions.

4. Are the powers more or less independent agents?

Yes. The powers tend not to be seen as part of a satanic hierarchy, although the powers may be seen as demonized or being "demonic" in given situations. Green represents a minority position in merging the demons and the powers.

5. Where is the activity of the powers a missiological concern?

The political arena. It is no surprise that discussions of the principalities and powers occur in Mott, Mouw, and Wink. The treatment of the powers in fact generally follows the lines laid down by Reformed theologies of institutions. The Reformed focus is not exclusively political, as Mott's titles (see below) or Mouw's call to expand the scope of the powers discussion (1979, 93) illustrate.

6. What is the paradigmatic form of spiritual warfare?

Political action. There are other forms as well, and the chapter titles in "Paths to justice," a section in Mott's *Biblical Ethics and Social Change* illustrate the range:

Evangelism

The church as counter-community

Strategic noncooperation

After all else—then arms?

Creative reform through politics

Wink would at least add "rooting out the violence within" and "exorcism," and "delete arms." Again, much from the liberation theologies would be relevant here.

7. Are the powers engaged directly in spiritual warfare?

Not generally, although Wink and Kellermann provide counter-examples.

8. Does spiritual warfare mean using a qualitatively different sort of power than our foes?

Given the Reformed option for just war and the use of political power, would it be fair to say that the Reformed tradition characteristically sees the same sort of power being used by church and world? Wink's discussion of the way of the Cross strikes a different note, but Wink is quite happy to use the political power generated by nonviolent actions.

This question needs a good deal more teasing out. How does the Cross relate to mission? Which sorts of power may be faithfully combined—and how? Does power (which sort?) (always? sometimes? never?) mean coercion or violence? Some ways forward, as well as the limitations of a simple Reformed/Anabaptist contrast are suggested by this excerpt from a Melbourne 1980 section report:

> The eye of faith discerns in that Cross the embodiment of a God who out-suffers, out-loves and out-lives the worst that powers do. In the decisive events which followed the crucifixion, something radically new happened which seems best described as a new creation. An altogether new quality of power appeared to be let loose among humankind (CWME 1980, 209).

9. Does spiritual warfare involve seeking to save the powers?

Yes. Berkhof talks about "christianizing" the powers, and this is implicit in Reformed social ethics as a whole. Wink calls for calling institutions back to their original vocation.

10. Does spiritual warfare call us into question in any fundamental way?

Both Linthicum's community organizing chart and Wink's discussion of finding the enemy within are examples of seeing that the enemy is not simply "out there." As with Pogo, we have met the enemy and he is us.

THREE

Over Against:
The Anabaptist Tradition

THE ANABAPTIST TRADITION contrasts the gospel and the power
mediated by social structures. The gospel means freedom from that
power. This stress affects mission design in both the church and the world.
In the church, it asks what a people truly free from the powers look like.
In their history, the Anabaptists have sought non-hierarchial forms of
church life. In the world, it offers other ways for the church to deal with
politics.

Gerhard and Norbert Lohfink

Gerhard Lohfink is a former professor of New Testament on the
Catholic Theological Faculty at the University of Tübingen, and a member
of "Integriete Gemeinde," a group of some seven hundred Munich Chris-
tians concerned with biblical, liturgical, and community renewal. Norbert
Lohfink, S.J., his brother, is Professor of Old Testament at Sankt Georgen,
Frankfurt-am-Main, and is strongly connected with the Integriete
Gemeinde as well.

In *Jesus and Community*, Gerhard Lohfink argues that God's goal
for Israel was to make it a contrast-society. Abraham's seed was to model
a common life marked by *shalom* and so be a blessing to the nations (Gen.
12:1-3). The nations would stream to Israel of their own accord (Isa. 2:2-3).
Jesus pursued this goal with the disciples and the church. How would the
church contrast with the world? By practicing brotherly love, erasing
social barriers, and by rejecting domination and violence.

How does this bear on our topic? The rejection of domination is
the clearest point of contact. Since God is the disciples' Father, that title is
not for others (Matt. 23:8-12). God as Father provides for the disciples
(Matt. 6:31-33), but will have no rivals. "If there no longer exist for them

[the disciples] the kind and caring fathers of the past, but only the one Father in heaven, then it is all the more true that authoritarian fathers exercising power have gone out of existence" (1984, 49). Jesus broadens the issue:

> You know that those who are supposed to rule over the Gentiles lord it over them, and their great men exercise authority over them. But it shall not be so among you; but whoever would be great among you must be your servant, and whoever would be first among you must be slave of all. For the Son of man also came not to be served but to serve, and to give his life as a ransom for many (Mk 10:42b-45).

The issue here, Lohfink contends, is structures of domination. These are standard for the world, but not for the disciples.

Lohfink comments briefly on these structures. Eph. 2:1-3 suggests that our societies carry the burden of pasts which are unresolved and unredeemed. From these too Christ must free us. Further, we are free not in a vacuum, but in the church. "The church is the place in which the freedom and reconciliation opened in principle by Christ must be lived in social concreteness" (1984, 145).

God's wisdom is made known to powers as the church is built up "as a society in contrast to the world, as the realm of Christ's rule in which fraternal love is the law of life" (1984, 145). It is in this context that Lohfink approaches the question of "signs and wonders."

> Christian communities today would do well to reflect on why wonders no longer occur in their midst—or why no one speaks of the wonders which do occur. Of course we have to speak of miracles today in a much more nuanced way than the early Christians did. . . . Nonetheless, when Christian communities are again transformed into true communities, wonders will begin anew (1984, 86-87).

What does this vision mean today? Besides *Jesus and Community*, a recent work by Norbert Lohfink, S.J., is relevant here. *Option for the Poor* shows that concern for the poor is commonplace in Israel's world. Stories abound with this pattern: people in distress, people crying to a god, the god hearing and seeing the distress, the god intervening (1987, 36). So the sequence of events in the Exodus story is not unique. What is unique —startling!—is that God intervenes by removing Israel from Egypt. Neither private acts of charity (Pharaoh's daughter saving Moses) nor counter-terror (Moses' slaying the Egyptian) do the job. Nor does reform (the compromises offered during Moses and Aaron's meetings with Pharaoh). Rather, God brings Israel out of Egypt—and at Sinai forms a new society, a contrast-society.

Here Lohfink engages many of the liberation theologians:

> One has the impression that, although they talk a lot about the Exodus, they do not really reckon, in the last analysis, with a genuine *departure* or *emigration* of the poor and with the emergence of a new society of emigrés. Their Moses does not, in a sense, stop negotiating with the Pharaoh; and one day he may well even become Minster of Culture, or some other high official in the Pharaoh's court . . . (1987, 51-52)

Rather, it is the basic ecclesiastical communities which are

> ...precisely what was envisioned as the goal of the Exodus credo in ancient Israel: places for social transformation. In them it is often really the case that the poor from country and barrio are assembled for a new life in contrast to all that went before, a life built on the memory of Israel and of Jesus (1987, 52).

Thus both Old and New Testaments invite us to respond to the powers with a contrast-society ruled by love and rejecting barriers, domination, and violence. Humanly speaking, impossible, but with God's power, possible.

John Howard Yoder

John Howard Yoder, president of Goshen Biblical Seminary, is a leading advocate of the Anabaptist ethical tradition. In *The Politics of Jesus,* Yoder argues that Jesus is both relevant and normative for Christian social ethics. In that context, he takes up the question of the principalities and powers. We will first sketch the general argument, and then turn to the powers.

The Politics of Jesus argues for this vision of Jesus:

> Jesus was not just a moralist whose teachings had some political implications; he was not primarily a teacher of spirituality whose public ministry unfortunately was seen in a political light; he was not just a sacrificial lamb preparing for his immolation, or a God-Man whose divine status calls us to disregard his humanity. Jesus was, in his divinely mandated (i.e. promised, anointed,

> messianic) prophethood, priesthood, and kingship, the
> bearer of a new possibility of human, social, and there-
> fore political relationships. His baptism is the inaugura-
> tion and his Cross is the culmination of that new regime
> in which his disciples are called to share (1972, 62-63).

These new relationships are marked by servanthood, forgiveness, and
nonviolence. (The list is almost identical to Gerhard Lohfink's.) This is an
option for private and public life, and an alternative to other options. "We
understand Jesus only if we can empathize with this threefold rejection:
the self-evident, axiomatic, sweeping rejection of both quietism and es-
tablishment responsibility, and the difficult, constantly reopened, genu-
inely attractive option of the crusade" (1972, 98).

This vision of Jesus is clearly relevant to our world; but is it
normative? Yes, argues Yoder. We are, for instance, called to forgive as
God has forgiven (Matt. 6:12f; Matt. 18:32f; Eph. 4:32; Col. 3:13) and to
love indiscriminately as God loves (Matt. 5:43-48; Luke 6:32-36). We are
called to love as Christ loved (John 13:34; 15:12; 1 John 3:11-16) and to
serve others as Christ served (John 13:1-17; Rom. 15:1-7; 2 Cor. 5:14ff;
8:7-9). In short, we are called to be "like Jesus" precisely "at the point of
the concrete social meaning of the Cross in its relation to enmity and
power. Servanthood replaces dominion, forgiveness absorbs hostility"
(1972, 134). To be a Christian is to live in this new world.

How does this relate to the principalities and powers? Yoder
begins his chapter "Christ and power" by summarizing Berkhof. The
powers are God's good creation, and they are fallen. Nevertheless, God
continues to preserve the world through them. Human lostness and
"survival are inseparable, both dependent upon the Powers" (1972, 146).

Jesus disarms, makes a public example of, and triumphs over the
powers (Col. 2:15). He does not destroy them, and here Yoder pushes
Berkhof's argument a step further:

> Man's subordination to these Powers is what makes him
> human, for if they did not exist there would be no history
> nor society nor humanity. If then God is going to save
> man *in his humanity*, the Powers cannot simply be de-
> stroyed or set aside or ignored (1972, 147).

While Yoder does not pursue this point, it is clear that here the issues of
the powers and of culture merge. The problems of contextualization and
syncretism are problems of dealing with the principalities and powers!

Returning to Yoder's argument, Jesus in the church proclaims this
victory over the powers. This victory is not proclaimed through special
actions by the church. It is proclaimed as the church "demonstrates in her

life and fellowship how men can live freed from the Powers" (Berkhof 1962, 42). Thus—still exegeting Berkhof—"the very existence of the church is her primary task" (1972, 153).

> What he [Paul] says is not . . . that the gospel deals only with personal ethics and not with social structures. Nor does he say that the only way to change structures is to change the heart of an individual man. . . . the primary social structure through which the gospel works to change other structures is that of the Christian community (1972, 157).

So how do we relate to these principalities and powers in the world? Yoder is giving two sorts of answers. The first answer is to point to the church as God's instrument for confronting the powers. This confrontation does not happen when the church as a political entity wields power in society. It happens when the church models a qualitatively different life in the midst of the society.

Second, our response is cruciform. "Only at one point, only on one subject—but then consistently, universally—is Jesus our example: in his Cross" (1972, 97).

Yoder's discussion of "revolutionary subordination" is relevant here. Yoder starts with the commands regarding husbands and wives, and masters and servants (e.g., Col. 3:18-4:1; Eph. 5:21-6:9; 1 Pet. 2:13-3:7). Many scholars see these as taken from the Stoics, an example of Jesus' ethic needing help from other sources. Yoder argues that these injunctions are grounded in Jesus' practice. These texts urge subordination because the gospel gives good grounds for thinking subordination irrelevant. The commands are given to both parties (wives and husbands, children and parents, etc.) which further erodes the "givenness" of the institutions.

> The wife or child or slave who can accept subordination because "it is fitting in the Lord" has not forsaken the radicality of the call of Jesus; it is precisely this attitude toward the structures of this world, this freedom from needing to smash them since they are about to crumble anyway, which Jesus had been the first to teach and in his suffering to concretize (1972, 192).

For Yoder, the questions of Christian identity and social ethics fall together. And the principalities and powers are right in the middle, as the preserving and destroying overlords of God's creation. Jesus engaged them by creating a new regime—and ended up on the Cross. The resurrection validates Jesus' path—also for his disciples. One example of this cruciform path is revolutionary subordination, the service of subordinates set free.

Vernard Eller

Vernard Eller is professor of Religion at the University of LaVerne in California. His *Christian Anarchy* might seem a bit out of place, until we recall that "anarchy" is formed from *"an"* ("un") + *"archy"* ("rule" or "principality"). Eller is assuming and building on the work of Berkhof, the Blumhardts, and Ellul, among others. Eller lays out the thesis at the start of his book:

> For us, then, "arky" identifies any principle of governance claiming to be of primal value for society. "Government" (that which is determined to *govern* human action and events) is a good synonym—as long as we are clear that political arkys are far from being the only "governments" around. Not at all; churches, schools, philosophies, ideologies, social standards, peer pressures, fads and fashions, advertising, planning techniques, psychological and sociological theories—all are arkys out to govern us.
>
> "Anarchy" ("unarkyness"), it follows, is simply the state of being unimpressed with, disinterested in, skeptical of, nonchalant toward, and uninfluenced by the highfalutin claims of any and all arkys. And "Christian Anarchy"— the special topic of this book—is a Christianly motivated "unarkyness." Precisely because Jesus is THE ARKY, the Prime of Creation, the Principal of All Good, the Prince of Peace and Everything Else, Christians dare never grant a human arky the primacy it claims for itself (1987, 1-2).

Lest this seem too abstract, it is hardly accidental that Eller's son Enten on reaching eighteen refused to register for military service. Eller recounts the ensuing events as one of his examples of what Christian anarchy looks like (see below).

Of the twelve principles for Christian anarchy Eller develops, six are of interest here:

1. For Christians, "anarchy" is never an end and goal in itself. The dying-off of arky (or our dying to arky) is of value only as a making of room for the Arky of God.

2. Christian anarchists do not even argue that anarchy is a viable option for secular society. Ellul: "Political authority and

organization are necessities of *social life* but *nothing more than necessities. . . ."*

3. Christian anarchists do not hold that the arkys, by nature, are "of the devil." . . . No, for Christian anarchists the problem with arkys is, rather, that they are "of the *human"*—i.e., they are creaturely, weak, ineffectual, not very smart, while at the same time they are extravagantly pretentious.

4. It is no part of Christian Anarchy to want to attack, subvert, unseat, or try to bring down any of the world's arkys. . .

5. . . .the radical-discipleship churches that have been most anarchist toward the state and the world may have the best track records regarding the loving of neighbors near and far and the serving of human need. Anarchism is no bar to social *service. . .*

6. Christian Anarchists occasionally are willing to work through and even use worldly arkys when they see a chance to accomplish some immediate human good thereby. This is an admittedly risky business; the regular pattern is to make a quick entrance and just as quick an exit (1987, 12-19).

Eller's principles offer a portrait of Christian anarchy which would be unrecognizable to anarchists as we traditionally think of them. The tenth principle, in particular, opens the door to working through institutions—on a selective basis.

What does this look like in practice? Eller cites a number of examples, starting with a contrast between Jacques Ellul and Dan West. Both were active in Spain during the Spanish Civil War. Ellul worked against Franco, but later judged that this accomplished nothing. West was working as the Brethren Service Commission representative. He was giving out food, but saw that a better response would be "to replenish the herds, flocks, hutches, cotes, and hives of the devastated areas of the world" (1987, 21). The result was Heifer Project International, whose work is characterized by strict political nonpartisanship. Ellul's judgment, argues Eller, would not apply here.

Eller thinks both Karl Barth and Dietrich Bonhoeffer often acted like Christian anarchists. The debate on Barth's politics is far from over, but two stories of Barth's dealings with the Nazis illustrate Eller's point.

Barth's first eyeball-to-eyeball confrontation with that regime came with the directive that all university classes were to open with the Hitler salute. Barth's never did. As he explained to the administration, he had understood it as being a "recommendation" rather than an "order." Besides, it was his custom to open class with a hymn and prayer—and the Hitler salute didn't seem to quite fit. The administration decided not to make an issue of the matter, and Barth carried the day on that one.

On the next go-around, Barth was not so fortunate. The university prescribed an "oath of loyalty to the Führer." And was our professor so defiant as to refuse? Of course not! "Granted, 'I did not refuse to give the official oath, but I stipulated an addition to the effect that I could be loyal to the Führer only within my responsibilities as an Evangelical Christian'." . . . Immediately suspended from teaching, by 1935 Barth was permanently "busted" from the university and had moved . . . back to Switzerland to finish his career there (Eller 1987, 139, citing Busch [citations omitted]).

Eller sees Paul's sending Onesimus back to Philemon as an exercise in Christian anarchy. Since Paul is pro-God, it is a secondary question whether he is pro- or anti-slavery.

The Onesimian approach is much the more powerful. It may take a while, but no slaveholder can forever hold out against the loving persuasions of a Paul, the loving self-sacrifice of an Onesimus, or the loving Spirit of an Almighty God. That owner actually has a much better chance of resisting political pressure and the violence of a class warfare. Moreover, the Onesimian way, rather than demanding the denunciation and destruction of the moral dignity of the slaveholder, offers him a gracious way out. Onesimus was liberated without Philemon's having to be demeaned in the process. Best of all, of course, to go Onesimian leaves everyone involved— slave, owner, and apostle—as brothers in Christ. The side effects are all positive, without a trace of contention's negativity.

This Onesimus is quite likely the one who became bishop of Ephesus—not a bad ending to the story!

Finally, Enten Eller. On reaching eighteen, Enten declined to register for the military draft (a felony, involving five years in prison and a $10,000 fine). Enten's decision not to register was not a matter of setting himself against the government. Even before being indicted he gave the government his summer itinerary; he did not seek the media spotlight as a way of gaining leverage; he declined to offer any defense besides his theological rationale for not registering. God's grace, attests Vernard Eller, was acting there, and resulted in the prosecution bending over backwards to affirm Enten's integrity. A veteran Associated Press reporter observed "This is the strangest trial I've ever seen" (1987, 262). Where Christian anarchy is practiced, argues Eller, it's possible that grace may spread farther than anyone would expect.

Summary

> And he came to Nazareth, where he had been brought up; and he went to the synagogue, as his custom was, on the sabbath day. And he stood up to read; and there was given to him the book of the prophet Isaiah. He opened the book and found the place where it was written, "The Spirit of the Lord is upon me, because he has anointed me to preach good news to the poor. He has sent me to proclaim release to the captives and recovering of sight to the blind, to set at liberty those who are oppressed, to proclaim the acceptable year of the Lord." And he closed the book, and gave it back to the attendant, and sat down; and the eyes of all in the synagogue were fixed on him. And he began to say to them, "Today this scripture has been fulfilled in your hearing" (Luke 4:16-21).

Interpreters have had difficulty, Yoder notes, deciding in what sense Jesus believed that Scripture had been fulfilled. But the event to which the Scripture points is, Yoder argues, clear: "a visible socio-political, economic restructuring of relations among the people of God, achieved by his intervention in the person of Jesus as the one Anointed and endued with the Spirit" (1972, 39). The conviction of the Lohfinks, Yoder, and Eller is that the fulfillment of this Scripture in the life of the church today is the starting point for any serious discussion of mission today in general, and of engaging the powers in particular.

Using the same questions that we used for the Reformed tradition, how does the Anabaptist tradition deal with the principalities and powers in mission?

1. To what texts does this tradition characteristically appeal?	Isa. 2:2-4 (the pilgrimage of the nations), Mark 10:42-45 (not lording it over each other, but service).

2. Are the powers personal spiritual beings?

Perhaps; Eller's reading of the New Testament suggests that we should at least treat them as though they were.

3. Are the powers integrally connected to cultures, societies, etc?

Yes. Yoder in fact takes Berkhof one step further at this point. As noted, studies of culture and mission may need to deal directly with the powers.

4. Are the powers more or less independent agents?

Yes, as with the Reformed tradition.

5. Where is the activity of the powers a missiological concern?

Wherever the powers are overreaching themselves. This is a rather wider sphere than that defined by the Reformed tradition.

6. What is the paradigmatic form of spiritual warfare?

The formation of a contrast-society (the church!) in the midst of the old structures of domination. The tension between this sort of claim and the ongoing sinfulness in the church is not one that is easily addressed. That it is a problem is evidenced by an otherwise splendid work from within the Anabaptist tradition which suggests that those concerned with justice find avenues other than the church through which to work.

7. Are the powers engaged directly in spiritual warfare?

No, but the Eller trial may be an example of the powers engaging us directly.

8. Does spiritual warfare mean using a qualitatively different sort of power than our foes?

Yes. The Eller trial is perhaps the clearest case.

9. Does spiritual warfare involve seeking to save the powers?

Indirectly, yes, in the pilgrimage of the nations to Jerusalem, for example.

10. Does spiritual warfare call us into question in any fundamental way?

Yes. We must change, and change before others do. Further, we do not judge the efficacy of the changes by whether they elicit changes in others.

FOUR

Expect a Miracle:
The Third Wave Tradition

THE THIRD WAVE seeks to recover the power of the gospel, particularly as evidenced by "signs and wonders" for (self-described) evangelicals. Whether faced with sickness, demon possession, besetting sins, or resistant people groups, the third wave would see God's salvation come in decisive and unambiguous ways.

A growing network of people in the third wave tradition are engaging in spiritual warfare against territorial spirits. This usually grows out of other ministries, such as evangelism or counseling. The presenters at the Spiritual Warfare Track at Lausanne II in Manila represent a short list of leaders:

- Ms. Rita Cabezas de Krumm, Ministerios Libertad, Costa Rica
- Ms. Neuza Itioka, O. C. Ministries, Brazil
- Dr. Charles Kraft, School of World Mission, Fuller Theological Seminary
- Dr. Edward F. Murphy, O. C. Ministries
- Rev. Edgardo Silvoso, Harvest Evangelism
- Dr. C. Peter Wagner, School of World Mission, Fuller Theological Seminary
- Rev. Tom White, Mantle of Praise Ministries

We will focus here on C. Peter Wagner, Tom White, John Dawson and Frank Peretti.

C. Peter Wagner

C. Peter Wagner, professor of mission at Fuller Theological Seminary's School of World Mission, is a leading missiologist in the church-growth tradition. His concern is world evangelization, which has lead him to deal first with signs and wonders, and now with territorial spirits. Wagner endorses the view of Timothy Warner, professor of mission at Trinity Evangelical Divinity School: "I have come to believe that Satan does indeed assign a demon or corps of demons to every geopolitical unit in the world, and that they are among the principalities and powers against whom we wrestle" (Wagner 1989, 278).

So the evangelist must learn spiritual warfare. This is supported by texts like Dan. 10, Acts 13:6-13, Eph. 6:12 and Matt. 12:29. This last text provides a key image: territorial spirits, like the strong man, can be bound and plundered.

The third wave tradition draws a lot of support from experience. For example, Wagner recounts stories that support this view of binding and plundering.

Thailand. A wave of conversions followed when the missionaries set aside one day a week for spiritual warfare.

Uruguay-Brazil border. People who were closed to the gospel on the Uruguay side of the town's main street became open when they crossed over to the Brazilian side.

Costa Rica. Symptoms of mental illness left a patient when she traveled to the United States, and they reappeared when she returned to Costa Rica. Christian psychologist Rita Cabezas was told by one of the demons that they were limited to their territory and could not go to the United States.

Navajo Reservation. Herman Williams, a Navajo Alliance pastor, suffered serious physical symptoms which left him as he crossed the reservation boundary for treatment in the city, and recurred when he entered the reservation again. The spirits causing this were traced to a witch doctor who was later killed by them.

Philippines. Lester Sumrall cast a spirit out of an inmate in Bilibid Prison, which was followed by a dramatic change in the receptivity of Filipinos to the gospel.

Argentina. Omar Cabrera, by prayer and fasting, exercises a ministry of identifying the spirits controlling certain cities, breaks their power, and finds little subsequent resistance to God's power for salvation and healing.

Korea. Paul Yonggi Cho attributes the contrast in receptivity to the gospel between Germany and Korea to the victories in spiritual warfare gained through the ministry of prayer of Korean Christians.

Argentina. Edgardo Silvoso reports the accelerated multiplication of churches within a radius of 100 miles of the city of Rosario after a team broke the power of the spirit of Merigildo in 1985 (1989, 282-83).

As some of the examples suggest, it may be important to identify spirits by name (see Mark 5:9). Wagner cites the work of Omar Cabrera and Rita Cabezas as examples. Rita Cabezas de Krumm of Ministerios Libertad (Costa Rica) gave a paper at Manila with an organizational chart for the powers. Anoritho's portfolio covers "abuse, adultery, drunkenness, fornication, gluttony, greed, homosexualism, lesbianism, lust, prostitution, seduction, sex, and vice" (Wagner 1989, 12). Clearly, this tradition offers the most detailed cosmology of all the traditions surveyed here. Again, Wagner cites Omar Cabrera:

> His general practice, after the potential site is selected, is to check into a hotel and seclude himself alone in a room in prayer and fasting. It usually takes the first two or thee days to allow the Holy Spirit to cleanse him, to help him disassociate from himself, and to identify with Jesus. He feels he "leaves the world" and is in another realm where the spiritual warfare takes place. The attacks of the enemy at times become fierce. He has even seen some spirits in physical form. His objective is to learn their names and break their power over the city. It usually takes five to eight days, but sometimes more. Once he spent 45 days in conflict. But when he finishes, people in his meetings frequently are saved and healed even before he preaches or prays for them (1988a, 199).

Wagner lists a number of dangers in spiritual warfare against these spirits. First, "engaging in meaningless rhetoric." Generic prayers of deliverance over cities are suspect. Second, "underestimating the enemy." "If you do not know what you are doing . . . Satan will eat you for breakfast." Third, "expecting power without prayer." Fourth, "overemphasizing power." Communicating the gospel "involves a delicate balance of weakness and power." Fifth, "ignorance" (1988b, 15-17).

Berkhof gave Japan as an example of a nation preserved but also separated from God by the powers; Wagner closes his 1988 paper by turning to Japan. Christian missionary efforts in Japan have yielded "perhaps the lowest return through the years of any nation of the world" (1988b, 18). "We have tried almost everything else. Why not try spiritual warfare" (1988b, 19)? The orientation is cheerfully pragmatic: faced with such challenges, why not try spiritual warfare?

Note that while Wagner's concern is evangelization, he recognizes that spiritual warfare encompasses a broader range of issues:

> Former Secretary of the Interior, James Watt, through sensitivities acquired in his past association with the

occult, perceives specific dark angels assigned to the White House. The implications that such insights could have for social justice, peace and national righteousness, to say nothing of evangelization, are obvious (1988b, 9).

Wagner is typical of this third wave tradition in that he shares with it four major beliefs:

1. The New Testament "principalities and powers" refer solely to evil spiritual beings. They may manifest themselves through institutions, natural phenomena, manufactured items, or human beings. Michael Green appears in Wagner's reader (1990) to buttress this point.

2. These beings control particular spheres, such as geographical territories, people groups, or particular sins. "But if the strong man (Satan) controls a house, could he not also control a nation, or city, or tribe?" (Wagner 1989, 280). Deut. 32:8, Dan. 10 and Acts 13:6-13 (Wagner 1989, 281-82) also come into play.

3. These beings hinder evangelism (2 Cor. 4:3-4). This is often the reason for the group's interest. At a recent meeting on this subject: "Consultation participants concurred that the ultimate goal of all spiritual warfare is the evangelization of the lost" (Rumph 1990, 11). Again, Tom White: *"the primary purpose of kingdom work is the writing of names in the book of life"* (1990, 133).

4. In any case success in evangelism depends on dealing directly with these beings. "The Key to victory is binding the 'Strong Man'" served as the title for a Wagner article (1986). He emphasizes 2 Cor. 10:4: "For the weapons of our warfare are not merely human, but they have divine power to destroy strongholds." One of the major open questions is in what cases, and how, one should deal with these beings.

Tom White

Tom White brings experience from some of the more esoteric elements of the 1960s counterculture. White is the founder of Mantle of Praise ministries (now Frontline Ministries) and has been teaching spiritual warfare on three levels: "boot camps" for laypeople, advanced training in discernment for pastors and missionaries, and strategic planning with other leaders.

White's paper for the Lausanne II Congress and recent book deserve attention. In them he urges caution in pursuing spiritual warfare, he proposes a quite substantial model for engaging in this warfare, and he stresses the importance of keeping spiritual warfare in perspective.

White's theme of caution reflects both his experience and a survey of Scripture. White finds no warrant for "a holy crusade designed to cleanse the heavens of pollutive powers of hell" (1989, 11). But White does not exclude direct confrontation with the powers, and he in fact devotes much of the paper to outlining a model for this.

Four stages are involved:

1. Separation (six months)
2. Shaping of Strategy (one year)
3. Mobilization (one year)
4. Evaluation and replication (six months)

Each stage is described in detail, and it is worth noting that a wide range of strategies is recommended in the second stage, including intercession, faith walks, doing justice, evangelism, deliverance ministries, and radical obedience. A focus on the powers can lead to the neglect of other dimensions, and White's model is a valiant attempt to avoid this neglect.

As for keeping spiritual warfare in perspective, White stresses that the extraordinary nature of this warfare should not short-circuit the ordinary: "The spontaneous, Spirit-led expansion of truth through the children of light is the normative means of advancing the kingdom. This will only occur in the context of bold, holy obedience."

Obedience is called for both inside and outside the church. "The greater triumph will come not by targeting and railing against evil powers, but by strengthening the church" (1990, 137). White tells of a training session for pastors in Taiwan on deliverance. They had named materialism as a major deity, and were at prayer. After a short period the prayer began to break up. White turned to the translator to find out what was going on.

> There were both mainlander and Taiwanese Chinese present, and strong feelings of hurt and hatred were surfacing that traced back to the struggle for Taiwan's independence. Suddenly, resentment, hatred and mistrust were confessed. The honest, painful exchange went on for several hours. There were tears of forgiveness and reconciliation. The Spirit was tending to priorities, mending the broken body. At first I left the room feeling rather defeated. "The body is just too self-occupied and divided to do this kind of praying." But as I reflected on the evening, the real meaning of Eph. 3:1-13 came to light.

> Here was the true victory, the miracle of reconciliation. This is what is to be "made known to the principalities and powers," and to the watching world—the supremacy of love that demonstrates the goodness and glory of God (1989, 28).

Outside the church, White argues:

> The practice of incarnational love that validates Jesus and liberates people from Satan's lies and bondage must be a centerpiece of spiritual warfare. No magical substitute exists for the sacrificial obedience of doing the will of God (1990, 139).

In a survey of models from church history White lifts up Charles Finney: "He possibly did more to purge our continent from evil than any other single man" (1989, 25). And Finney is an example of the importance of the ordinary emphases in mission. "In the context of our study, the striking point is that neither Wesley or Finney majored on dealing directly with the devil. They majored on obedience to truth, labor in prayer, and dependence on the Spirit" (1989, 25).

White's *The Believer's Guide to Spiritual Warfare* deals largely with questions of demonic activity directed towards the individual. But there is also some discussion of the principalities and powers as they affect societies and institutions. In addition to the points contained in his 1989 paper, his comments on the origin of the powers are of interest here.

Where did the powers come from? White notes three theories: "disembodied spirits of a pre-Adamic race . . . 'the Nephilim' of Genesis 6 . . . the original angelic creation that fell with Lucifer" (1990, 32). White's position is closest to the third, although he sees the powers as rebelling over a period of time. For this point he cites D. S. Russell's *The Method and Message of Jewish Apocalyptic*:

> There gradually grew up, no doubt under the influence of foreign [Persian] thought, the notion that the angels to whom God had given authority over the nations . . . had outstripped their rightful authority and had taken the power into their own hands (Russell 1964, 237-38, cited in White 1990, 33).

Notice that what Russell describes as a change in Jewish theology, White takes as real events in cosmic history.

John Dawson

John Dawson is the Southwest U.S. Director of Youth with a Mission (YWAM). One of the participants in the Pasadena Consultation, he is author of *Taking our Cities for God: How to Break Spiritual Strongholds* (1989). Dawson's themes are broadly within the third wave tradition, and also illustrate its diversity.

Dawson approaches mission primarily in terms of evangelism and ministries related to evangelism. This is in line with "the rightly prioritized agenda of a biblical believer," namely, "personal repentance and holy living, leading to united prayer, to revival of the church, to awakening among the lost, to reformation of society and international missionary endeavor" (1989, 136).

Mission in cities requires spiritual warfare, because "high-ranking, supernatural personalities, referred to as principalities and powers in Ephesians 6, seek to dominate geographic areas, cities, peoples and subcultures" (1989, 137). This is a different statement of how the powers and, say, cities relate than we have met previously. In both the Reformed and Anabaptist traditions, as well as in some third wave writers, the powers are seen as integrally related to areas, institutions, or whatever. For Dawson, the relationship is much looser. Dawson argues that God, not the powers, is responsible for cultural and geographic divisions (1989, 157). This too contrasts with the rather tighter relationship previously pictured between the powers and human cultures. This may be a strength in Dawson's model; the more loosely the powers are connected to our cities, the less problematic it is to take these cities for God. But there are clearly different perceptions of how the powers and institutions relate.

Angels, Dawson argues, are also assigned to particular geographical regions. From the Old Testament, Dawson cites Ezek. 9:1 and Dan. 12:1; from the New Testament, Acts 10:30 and 16:9.

Personal repentance heads Dawson's agenda, and this is directly connected with spiritual warfare:

> There is a battle raging over your city and it is affecting you right now. Our individual blind spots and vices are usually common to the culture around us, and that culture is influenced by what the Bible calls principalities and powers (Eph. 6). In other words, you are being buffeted by the same temptations as others around you. (1989, 27-28)

Therefore, repentance—dealing with one's own complicity in the evil that is attacking the city—is the first step. This is evident in Dawson's account of a YWAM evangelistic effort in Cordoba, Argentina in 1978. When their first efforts yielded no fruit, the team fasted and prayed. God, reports Dawson, answered by revealing both the city's nature—proud and beautiful—and a strategy: humility. "We were discerning a principality attempting to rule the city in the pride of life, so we had to confront it in an opposite spirit with a strategy of personal humility" (1989, 19).

> We went downtown the next day—all two hundred of us—and formed into small groups of about thirty. We positioned ourselves all through the fashionable malls and streets for pedestrians of the downtown area. Then we did it. We knelt down right there in the midst of the fashion parade, surrounded by expensive bistros, outdoor cafes and boutiques. With our foreheads to the cobblestones, we prayed for a revelation of Jesus to come to the city (1989, 19).

They got a hearing. And Dawson makes it clear that it was not only the pride of the city, but the pride of the YWAM team which had to be addressed.

Dawson, who repeatedly stresses the role of the Spirit, also stresses homework. If we are going to take a city for God, we need to know something about it. Dawson devotes four chapters to "essential research in the areas of history, covenants, current revelation and demographics" (1989, 75). For instance:

- History: Why is the city there? What dreams created it? Nurtured it? What battles have been fought here? What has been born here? What is the history of the various ethno-linguistic groups?
- Covenants: What has God been doing with the church? The Christian worker should know the history of the church in the nation and in the city. They should know its history in ministry to the particular group in question, the history of the sort of mission being carried out, and the history of their own movement.
- Current revelation: Be aware of what God is doing with the church now, cooperate with believers from fellowships other than your own.
- Demographics: A question not only about the present, but about the future. Dawson provides "Toward 2000: Eighteen trends in L.A." as an example.

And what does spiritual warfare look like after all this work? Dawson proposes that the five steps to victory are:

1. Worship: The place of beginnings
2. Waiting on the Lord for insight
3. Identifying with the sins of the city
4. Overcoming evil with good
5. Travailing until birth

The third step recalls Dawson's earlier emphasis on repentance. The Cordoba story provides one example of the fourth step. Others: Dawson's freely sharing YWAM's mailing list to break down fear and suspicion among Christians or his "taking authority" over the fate of an airplane. The fifth step suggests process, rather than a clean-cut event.

Frank Peretti

Frank Peretti's novels *This Present Darkness* (1986) and *Piercing the Darkness* (1989) reflect the third wave tradition. The books are popular; the former is in its 28th printing, the latter in its 6th. While Peretti describes his approach as "a creative fictional treatment on a theme," he argues that the books reflect our world: "The reality I am talking about in my book is not just entertainment or diversion or fairy tale. People who have read my book tell me that what I wrote about is happening in their towns *right now*" (1990, 8-9).

This Present Darkness tells how a small town is saved from a global satanic conspiracy through the efforts of both humans and angels. The conspiracy tries to bring people under various forms of demonic domination under the guise of channeling, spirit guides, and other New Age activities.

The opposing forces consist of both spirits and humans. On the satanic side, there are demons identified with particular sins. As one ascends the hierarchy, we meet Lucius the Prince of Ashton (the town in question), Rafar the Prince of Babylon, and the Strongman (from the head office). There is constant infighting among these powers, which is one reason for their final defeat. Among the humans, the local heavy is Professor Juleen Langstrat, a UCLA graduate whose interests lie in psychology's marshlands. On the angelic side, many are pictured in territorial terms: "Nathan, the towering Arabian who fought fiercely and spoke little. It was he who had taken demons by their ankles and used them as warclubs against their fellows" (1986, 44). The leaders: Tal the Captain of the Host, Guilo, and the General. Among the humans, Henry L. Busche, a fundamentalist minister, and Marshall Hogan, the editor/owner of the local paper. The humans save the town largely by praying; the angels by combat.

What does prayer do? Prayer empowers angels, disempowers demons.

> "Tal took a quick survey of the prayer cover he had
> gathered. It had to be enough for tonight's plan to work"
> (1986, 256). "He could feel his strength building with the
> prayers of the saints; his sword began to burn with
> power, glowing brilliantly" (1986, 261). "'What is Rafar
> lord of?' 'Rafar is lord of Ashton. Rafar rules Ashton.' . .
> 'Well, we rebuke him too!' said Ron. Near the big dead
> tree, Rafar spun quickly around as if someone had just
> pricked him, and he eyed several of his demons suspi-
> ciously" (1986, 242).

As in the example, the disempowering effect increases if the demon's
name is used.

The angels save the town by combat, as spiritual warfare is pictured as physical:

> Guilo returned the blow, their swords locked for a mo-
> ment, arm against arm, and then Guilo made good use
> of his foot to cave in the demon's face and sent it tumbling
> out over the canyon (1986, 267).

"Obviously," says Peretti, "I used familiar images like sword play to
illustrate warfare" (1990, 8). But we are apparently to take the role of
prayer and the conflict between angels and demons at face value.

People may be controlled to various degrees by demons. Most of
the time this is part of a larger strategy for the town. The demons may be
exorcised by commands, often in Jesus' name.

What vision of good and evil undergirds the book? The theological
lines are drawn clearly. The fundamentalists wear the white hats. The
values are traditional, as in the descriptions of Mary, the pastor's wife:

> . . . but she was a terrific support for him, always there,
> always believing God for the best and always believing
> in Hank too (1986, 24), "this flower sitting at the piano is
> my wife, Mary." Mary stood quickly, smiled meekly,
> then sat down again (1986, 171).

And the villains? One pastor is described as "'just a little too cush, you
know? He's into all this family of man stuff, discovering yourself, saving
the whales . . .'" (1986, 65). At one point, one of the demonic front
organizations is being described: "You wouldn't believe how influential
they are in Arab oil, the Common Market, the World Bank, international
terrorism—" (1986, 205). The four are, the text implies, on the same level.

In the middle is the town. Peretti introduces it like this:

> It was the time of the Ashton Summer Festival, the town's yearly exercise in frivolity and chaos, its way of saying thank you, come again, good luck, and nice to have you to the eight hundred or so college students at Whitmore College who would be getting their long awaited summer break from classes. Most would pack up and go home, but all would definitely stay at least long enough to take in the festivities, the street disco, the carnival rides, the nickel movies, and whatever else could be had, over or under the table, for kicks. It was a wild time, a chance to get drunk, pregnant, beat up, ripped off, and sick, all in the same night (1986, 9).

Peretti is concerned that the angels not lose the battle over this town, but what he finds to enjoy or value in the town is less clear.

Part of the story is Hank learning how spiritual warfare works. As the reader watches Hank learn, the reader learns as well. It is a question not only of learning about prayer, but of learning God's priorities: "Hank grew more determined to stay in the battle and give Satan a real run for his money. He was sure that was what God wanted" (1986, 64).

Summary

Returning to our questions, what responses does the third wave tradition give?

1. To what texts does this tradition characteristically appeal?

   Matt. 12:29 (binding the strong man), Eph. 6:12 (the nature of our struggle).

2. Are the powers personal spiritual beings?

   Yes. Yet White's use of D. S. Russell raises a key question. Russell argues that Jewish belief in the powers was a response to Jewish theological problems: God's transcendence and the problem of evil. To the degree that third wave practitioners buy into this worldview —e.g., Rita Cabezas' organizational charts—they need to wrestle with its historically conditioned nature. This is, of course, a challenge for all the traditions, but appears in its most acute form here.

3. Are the powers integrally connected to cultures, societies, etc?

Some people within this tradition assume the work of thinkers like Berkhof, and so would give a positive response. Others, like Dawson and Peretti, picture the powers as more loosely related to groups or institutions. It would appear that this latter position fits better with the images of binding or exorcism. In any case, more work may be needed. Exegetical backing for seeing the powers as integrally connected is available from the Reformed tradition; similar backing for seeing them as more loosely connected has not yet been provided.

4. Are the powers more or less independent agents?

No. They are part of a satanic hierarchy.

5. Where is the activity of the powers a missiological concern?

Where evil is encountered, as in resistance to the preaching of the gospel.

Peretti's novels are important here, for they merge advocacy of spiritual warfare with advocacy of cultural and religious traditionalism. We observed this in the vision of good and evil undergirding the book; Calvin Miller comes at the issue this way:

> There is a kind of spiritual McCarthyism smoldering in some evangelical circles where anyone who is disagreed with or who is considered "liberal" is regarded as being New Age. A book

like Peretti's certainly doesn't discourage that kind of McCarthyism. . . . [*This Present Darkness*] speaks to our worst fears (1990, 12).

The issue for the third wave tradition is the degree to which Peretti will turn out to be representative. In fairness to Peretti, this problem of parochial agendas is hardly confined either to him or to the third wave tradition.

6. What is the paradigmatic form of spiritual warfare?

Evangelism. Prayer or exorcism could equally well be put here.

7. Are the powers engaged directly in spiritual warfare?

Yes. Behind this simple affirmative there is a great deal of debate.

Under what circumstances does one deal with these beings? Sterk reports that John Wimber "feels that it is unwise to intentionally seek confrontation with territorial spirits, especially on the level of 'principalities,' because he feels that we have no Scriptural mandate to do so" (1989, 24).

Tom White has argued: "The direct exposing and dealing with higher powers of evil should only occur in the context of setting individual souls free from the grip of darkness. . . . As the Spirit guides, it is an imperative point of spiritual warfare that we *do not go looking for this level of battle, but that we let it find us*" (1989, 6).

How does one deal with these beings? White (1989) reports attending prayer meetings in 1985 and 1986 "petitioning the Lord to weaken the grip of the spiritual force standing behind the Rajneesh commune" (1989, 3) in Oregon. The commune closed in 1987. Edgardo Silvoso describes the experience of Eduardo Lorenzo in Adrogue (Argentina) in terms of "taking authority" over the chief demon (Silvoso 1989, 5).

8. Does spiritual warfare mean using a qualitatively different sort of power than our foes?

No. Peretti's angels and demons fight with the same weapons, and both enjoy a good fight. On the other hand, Wagner's comment that evangelism involves "a delicate balance of weakness and power" (1988b, 16) is relevant here.

9. Does spiritual warfare involve seeking to save the powers?

No. Peretti's demons are cheerfully dispatched into outer darkness.

10. Does spiritual warfare call us into question in any fundamental way?

Generally not, although Dawson's emphasis on repentance or White's story of the Taiwan seminar provide examples of being called into question fundamentally.

FIVE

Sociological Bible:
The Social Science Tradition

THE SOCIAL SCIENCE TRADITION touches on our topic at many points. There would be value in surveying these points broadly. Here our concern is more narrow: the suggestions of some Christians who work at these intersections in psychology and anthropology. There is a much internal diversity here. There are also different sorts of cross-links. These people could easily be treated in two or three chapters in a number of combinations. (Hiebert and Kelsey are influenced by Carl Jung; Hiebert and Shuster are evangelicals, associated with Fuller Theological Seminary.)

Morton Kelsey

Morton Kelsey is professor emeritus at Notre Dame University, whose writings on spirituality have been highly acclaimed. Our discussion here is based on "The Reality of a Spiritual World: the Demonic and Angelic Re-examined," an essay in *Discernment: A Study in Ecstasy and Evil*. We focus on Kelsey's reading of the powers as archetypes, and his proposal for the way in which these powers or archetypes are related to the human being.

Kelsey sees depth psychology as a way of bringing faith, reason, and experience together. Depth psychology's autonomous complexes and archetypes point to the same experience as the New Testament's angels and demons. This is a major claim; Kelsey backs it by a historical survey from Jesus to Jung, with Aquinas playing the pivotal role.

Jesus' understanding of people, Kelsey argues, is linked with his understanding of this spiritual realm. His understanding contrasts with ours. We often think that being human is a relatively straightforward affair: if we really want to, we can control ourselves and do what we wish.

Our courts and schools work on this assumption (1978, 62). Jesus believed that people could be influenced to varying degrees by both good and evil spiritual powers.

> He also spoke of achieving the single eye, implying that human beings could be other than single-eyed, single-minded, that there might be more than one center of personality and will within an individual, and that one of them could well be demonic or divine. He also spoke again and again ... of losing one's life to find it. Whatever else this means, it certainly implies that there are various levels of personality and that to gain one of them another has to be sacrificed.... One has to give up one's own will so that God's will (in other words, God's spirit or the Holy Spirit) can become the center of one's life and personality. The human will or ego cannot stand against demonic infiltration and possession unless one is endowed by the Spirit of God which protects a person (1978, 64).

We are necessarily linked to the spiritual realm, but this is good news or bad news depending on the link involved!

Kelsey moves to the apostles and church fathers, arguing that however they named these threats to the human person (demons, principalities), they saw that Christ came to rescue us from them (1978, 66). Moving further, Aquinas' definition of angels is *intelligibilia intelligentia* ("thinking thoughts" (1978, 70). Here, claims Kelsey, we are not far from "Jung's definition of unconscious complexes as 'groups of psychic contents, isolated from consciousness, functioning arbitrarily and autonomously, leading thus a life of their own in the unconscious; whence they can at any moment hinder or further conscious acts'" (Kelsey 1978, 71, citing Jung).

> The definition might be a very good description of Thomist devils—or angels. ...Our contention is that the meanings of the two sets of terms (the theological and the psychopathological) are, however, not mutually exclusive; and we would offer for expert consideration the suggestion that, while the meanings are different, each term may be, and commonly is, referable to the selfsame phenomenon or occurrence (White, cited in Kelsey 1978, 71).

Much of this is captured in Kelsey's diagram on the next page. Reality is divided into space-time and unconscious experience; the psyche (soul) lives largely in the realm of the unconscious. It is subject to the influence of spiritual beings (archetypes). Only God's action can preserve the psyche. (The relation between "The Holy Spirit of the Self" and "The Risen Christ or Holy Spirit," the caption appearing in a similar diagram [1976, 37] is not entirely clear. More complete diagrams appear in *Reaching*, 29 and 59.)

What do Kelsey's proposals mean for mission? First, if we live largely in the realm of the unconscious, we have a further reason for needing a healthy spirituality. This is a theme we've already met in Dawson's suggestion that the powers at work "out there" are also liable to be at work within.

Second, the relation of the self to these archetypes turns out to be complex. In "Psychology, religion, and discernment," another essay in *Discernment*, Kelsey offers a picture of the soul which houses Aphrodite, Ares, Demeter, Eros, Hephaestos, Hermes, Zeus, the Fool and Science.

> These nine men and women who have come to my door were neutral parts of me. If they are under the direction of wholeness and harmony, the master, the Risen Christ, then they work together. If they are left alone they quarrel and cause chaos. But worst of all they can fall into the hands of the Evil One. His stratagem is to convince each one that he or she is the only valuable person within and should subject the others to him or her (1978, 119-20).

The same archetypes structure both societies and the individual person. On the individual level, do we talk about a spirit of lust, or about Aphrodite gone astray? Do we seek exorcism or reintegration (or both)? This is one of the questions Kelsey's model poses. It should be noted that this is a question which can be addressed on both the individual and community levels. Kelsey develops the model for the individual, but when it is transposed to the community level, it dovetails with the Reformed concern for redeeming the powers.

Paul Hiebert

Paul Hiebert, formerly at Fuller Theological Seminary's School of World Mission, now serves as chair of the Department of Mission and Evangelism at Trinity Evangelical Divinity School.

Hiebert begins with his experience as a missionary in India. There popular religion explains illness by appealing to the spirit world, and deals with it by using magic or religion. The Christian response is often

Morton Kelsey's model

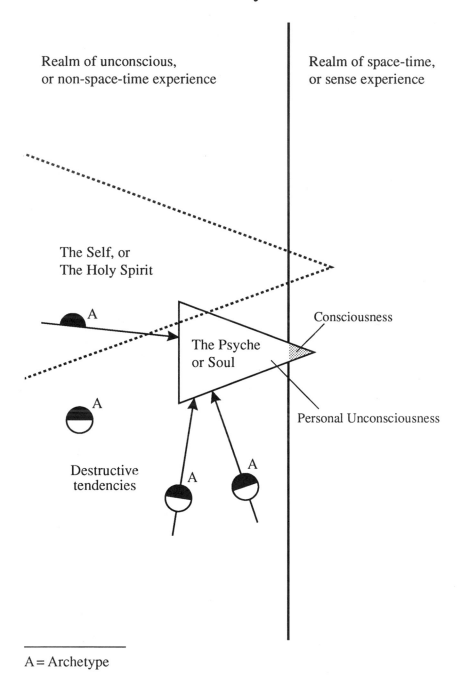

Realm of unconscious,
or non-space-time experience

Realm of space-time,
or sense experience

The Self, or
The Holy Spirit

A

Consciousness

The Psyche
or Soul

Destructive
tendencies

A

A

A

Personal Unconsciousness

A = Archetype

to deny the reality of the spirit world, and to rely on modern medicine. But often Christians go to witchdoctors or other mediums when faced with sickness. This is a major pastoral problem in the two-thirds world. Is there a more adequate response?

To start with, Hiebert suggests, we need to attend to the way we map, or describe, our world. Hiebert suggests two dimensions for any map: immanence-transcendence (seen vs. unseen or this-worldly vs. other-worldly) and organic-mechanical (living world vs. mechanical world). The immanence-transcendence axis runs from our familiar world to the unseen world independent of our world (the high gods). In the middle is the unseen world connected with our world inhabited by lesser beings: trolls, brownies, fairies, ancestors, territorial spirits. The modern west is rather abnormal in believing the middle realm to be empty. Anyhow, there are three possible realms here. The second axis, organic-mechanical, explains our experience in terms of living beings such as gods and spirits or in terms of impersonal processes such as the law of gravity, fate, or karma. Combined, these two axes yield the chart on the next page.

Each realm has its own questions. The upper realm deals with questions like the problem of suffering. The lower realm deals with questions like the conditions under which airplanes crash (loss of power, structural integrity). The middle realm deals with questions like "Will the plane I'm on now crash?"

The chart provides a framework for mapping different religious systems or worldviews. It makes no claims as to what is really out there, or how the world works. Folk religions focus on the middle world of demons, spirits, magic and witchdoctors. Some "higher religions" primarily address the unseen spiritual world. Modern science addresses the "real world," denying the reality of the middle realm (generally) or the realm of the high gods (sometimes). Hiebert summarizes:

> As a scientist I had been trained to deal with the empirical world in naturalistic terms. As a theologian, I was taught to answer ultimate questions in theistic terms. For me the middle zone did not really exist. Unlike Indian villagers, I had given little thought to spirits of this world, to local ancestors and ghosts, or to the souls of animals. For me these belonged to the realm of fairies, trolls and other mythical beings. Consequently I had no answers to the questions they raised (Hiebert 1982, 43).

No surprise, then, with Newbigin, that "Western Christian missions have been one of the greatest secularizing forces in history" (1982, 44).

FRAMEWORK FOR THE ANALYSIS OF RELIGIOUS SYSTEMS

ORGANIC ANALOGY
Based on concepts of living beings relating to other living beings. Stresses life, personality, relationships, functions, health, disease, choice, etc. Relationships are essentially moral in character.

MECHANICAL ANALOGY
Based on concepts of impersonal objects controlled by forces. Stresses impersonal, mechanistic and deterministic nature of events. Forces are essentially amoral in character.

UNSEEN or SUPERNATURAL
Beyond immediate sense experience. Above natural explanation. Knowledge of this based on inference or on supernatural experiences.

High Religion Based on Cosmic Beings: cosmic gods angels demons spirits of other worlds	*High Religion Based on Cosmic Forces:* kismet fate Brahman and karma impersonal cosmic forces
Folk or Low Religion local gods and goddesses ancestors and ghosts spirits demons and evil spirits dead saints	*Magic and Astrology* mana astrological forces charms, amulets and magical rites evil eye, evil tongue
Folk Social Science interaction of living beings such as humans, possibly animals and plants.	*Folk Natural Science* interaction of natural objects based on natural forces

OTHER WORLDLY
Sees entities and events occurring in some other worlds and in other times.

THIS WORLDLY
Sees entities and events as occurring in this world and universe.

SEEN or EMPIRICAL
Directly observable by the senses. Knowledge based on experimentation and observation.

What we need, as Hiebert suggests in the following chart, is a theology capable of dealing with all three areas.

A HOLISTIC THEOLOGY

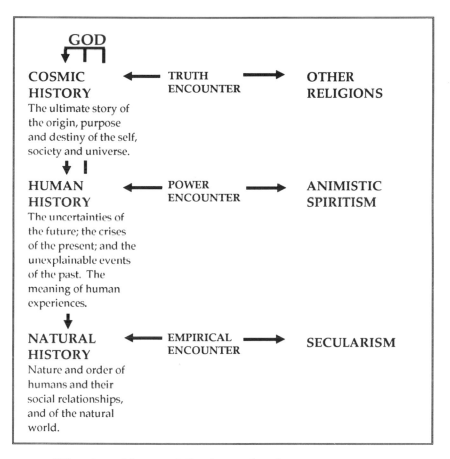

What does this mean? On the one hand,

> On the middle level, a holistic theology includes a theology of God in human history: in the affairs of nations, of peoples and of individuals. This must include a theology of divine guidance, provision and healing; of ancestors, spirits and invisible powers of this world; and of suffering, misfortune and death (1982, 46).

In principle, then, we cannot exclude the possibility of ancestors, spirits, and invisible powers working in our world. This is, however, simply the start of the conversation. To be open in principle to spirits does not mean to be credulous.

On the other hand, this does not mean turning Christianity into magic. To have a theology of the middle level does not mean that we control the middle level. Middle level affairs are in God's hands. Hiebert makes this point by telling the story of Yellayya, an Indian Christian leader who prayed for a Christian girl with smallpox. The child died, but weeks later Yellayya recounted:

> "The village would have acknowledged the power of our God had he healed the child, but they knew in the end she was mortal and eventually would have to die. When they saw in the funeral our hope of resurrection and reunion in heaven, they saw an even greater victory, over death itself, and they have begun to ask about the Christian way" (1982, 47).

Hiebert is currently addressing a number of other issues which bear on our subject: paradigms of spiritual warfare, types of power encounters, and the task of sorting out appearance and reality. Hiebert addresses the first two issues as both an anthropologist and a member of the Anabaptist tradition.

There are two paradigms of spiritual warfare to take into account. The following figure charts their differing placement of the actors. The first, the Indo-European paradigm, is laid out on the left. The second, the Judeo-Christian paradigm, is laid out on the right.

INDO-EUROPEAN			JUDEO-CHRISTIAN	
		Creator	GOD	
Spiritual realm	Gods vs. demons	*Creation (heavenly)*	Angels	Demons
Natural realm	Good vs. evil humans	*Creation (earthly)*	Organizations, Individuals Personality aspects	

In the Indo-European model there are two realms, the spiritual and natural. Both realms have good and evil inhabitants. In the Judeo-Christian model, God the Creator stands over against creation, which is divided into the heavenly and earthly. There is no evil counterpart to God. In the Indo-European model, humans are caught up in the battles between the gods: when the elephants play, the mice are trampled. In the Judeo-Christian model, God and the heavenly realm are trying to influence the earthly creation, whether human structures, human beings, or even the parts of the human personality (e.g., as described by Kelsey).

These two paradigms also contrast in the sort of conflict they envision. We all know the Indo-European paradigm: order is broken by the violence of an evil agent; a good agent uses more effective violence to restore order. This is the plot for detective stories and most war stories. We meet it in books, movies, stage and TV. By means of the following table, Hiebert suggests that the Judeo-Christian paradigm is very different.

CONTRASTING BATTLE PARADIGMS

	INDO-EUROPEAN	*JUDEO-CHRISTIAN*
Primary threat	Chaos (opposition)	Sin, rebellion
Primary goal	Order (law, cleanness)	Justice, righteousness
Secondary goal	Justice, righteousness	Order (law, cleanness)
Progression	Disorder > Order > Relationship	Lack of relationship > Relationship (& disorder)> Order
Object	Win battle; destroy enemy	Win the enemy
Power exercised through	Force	Influence, love
Stance towards enemy	Hate	Love
Analogy	War	Rebellious child
Divine role	Warrior	Parent
Symbol	Sword	Cross
Assumption	We must gain control	God is in control

In the Indo-European model, since the primary problem is chaos, the primary goal is order. We can achieve this order by gaining control of the situation by defeating our enemies. Once we establish order, we can address other issues such as justice. In the Judeo-Christian model, since the primary problem is sin, the primary goal is righteousness (justice). Once that is secured, other issues (order) can be addressed. Both models value justice and order, but they prioritize them differently.

In the Indo-European model, the battle is symmetrical: both agents seek victory through force. In the Judeo-Christian model, the battle is asymmetrical. The rebels are not so much trying to defeat God through force, as to co-opt or seduce God into acting as they do. (As the child may egg the parent on into losing control.) God, on the other hand, continues to act in love toward the rebels.

Our problem, argues Hiebert, is that we tend to read the Bible's story through Indo-European eyes, and miss these contrasts. For example, Peretti's novels are excellent examples of seeing spiritual warfare in Indo-European terms.

Hiebert is also working on developing a typology of power encounters. How do we understand these in terms of a Judeo-Christian battle paradigm? (And Hiebert is here clearly continuing to push the theological envelope.) The term "power encounter" can be used in two rather different ways.

Allan Tippett coined the term to describe the experience of a new convert who burns his or her idols or fetishes. Will the convert die or live? Here the missionary is only incidentally part of the encounter.

Elijah's encounter with the prophets of Baal (1 Kings 18) serves as a second paradigm. The paradigm is often thought of as "power encounter leads to victory, which leads to many believing." A closer look at the text (1 Kings 18-19) suggests a more ambiguous pattern: "power encounter leads to victory, which leads to rising opposition and some believing." Hiebert claims that this pattern in fact better represents the power encounters in Acts, where both persecution and belief tend to follow the power encounters.

With Christ and the Cross, the second paradigm is most profound —and ambiguous. In Matthew's gospel, the Cross is understood in legal terms. Jesus is executed by the powers. The resurrection is a sort of review by a higher court, which finds the lower court decision not simply wrong, but done with criminal intent. Hence the lower court loses its legitimacy.

John's gospel works with a power-encounter model, but in an ironic mode. Jesus poses his challenge via signs, but the signs do not lead to belief in any straightforward way. The Cross is the power encounter par excellence. Satan appears to win the first round, Jesus, through the resurrection, the second. While this can be read in terms of the Indo-European paradigm (victory after an initial defeat), something different is happening. Jesus rises from the dead and has nothing to say regarding Satan. Satan is still running around. There is power, but it's power of the Cross: we can take anything without giving up who we are. The rebel uses violence; we use law. Again, 10,000 angels could have come down, but that would have been a defeat. Jesus is always working towards reconciliation.

This reading of power encounters serves to flesh out the meaning of the Judeo-Christian battle paradigm. The way of battle is the way of the Cross.

Finally, regarding spirits, we need to take both phenomenology (appearances, or the beliefs of those we're dealing with) and ontology (reality) into account. Here we need to start with our own beliefs. We often assume that a spirit is a personal, autonomous being. This contrasts with the Bible's use of *ruah* (OT) or *pneuma* (NT), in which "spirit" is used more broadly (a spirit of truth, lying, and so on), rather like "ethos." This broader (biblical) use is probably more useful for us. So, with Wink, we can talk about the spirit of Nairobi without implying a personal being. Again, the *stoicheia* can be thought of as the basic drives or forces as work in human experience. These are often deified, both in their helpful and harmful aspects (sex, power, thrill, wealth). Here Hiebert and Kelsey move in the same direction.

In sorting out appearance and reality, Hiebert suggests a three-step process of investigation:

Phenomenology	What do people think is going on?
Ontology	What is really going on? This involves both science and theology. The combination (science and theology) is hardly simple, but it cannot be avoided.
Missiology	How to bring people from where they are to where they should be?

Missiology deals with both the short-range and with the long-range issues. For the immediate symptoms (the short-range), the approach is phenomenological: "Christ delivers you from all real and imagined demons." For the long-range, the approach must deal with ultimate causes. The danger here is to simply accept the people's phenomenological description of a phenomenon as a description of the reality itself.

These observations on the powers underscore how much work is still needed. We have to sort out our own assumptions. We need to attend to the difference between speaking about appearances (phenomenology) versus talking about reality (ontology). When is the Bible speaking phenomenologically? When is it speaking ontologically? And we need to deal with these questions in dialogue with multiple cultures.

Marguerite Shuster

Marguerite Shuster is the pastor of Knox Presbyterian Church in Pasadena, California. She wrote *Power, Pathology, Paradox: The Dynamics of Evil and Good* in response to both classic theological problems (particularly the nature of the person, and the relationship between the material and immaterial worlds) and the practical challenge of doing Christian counseling. How does one tell when the tools of psychology and other social sciences are no longer adequate? Under what conditions does one begin considering exorcism? How, in short, can the languages of theology and psychology be combined in a way that will aid the counselor? While this is similar in many respects to Kelsey's problem, Shuster comes at it in a rather different way.

In the chapter whimsically titled "The Nature of everything—with special reference to power," Shuster offers a model to account for everything from biofeedback and Psi phenomena to possession and sanctification. Shuster focuses on the sort of power that is "the ability to control or influence others," suggesting that it consists in *"a union of structure and will"* (1987, 95). This is not the way we usually think of power, but it does fit our experience.

> Now I clearly do not have *power* to go to the store unless both *structure* (path to the store, means of transportation, and enough cerebral neurons to keep the necessary sequence of actions in order) and *will* (perceived possibility and decision) are available and operative (1987, 96).

The necessity of both structure and will operating properly is expressed more simply by a line from the American TV show, *The Equalizer*: "Why break a man's kneecaps when you can mess with his mind?"

Still on the issue of power, on most levels, whether individual, national, or international, we tend to see power as the solution to any problem. If we just had more power . . . Yet if we only attend to the issue of power, we face two problems. First, the temptation to reductionism is virtually overwhelming. Given the multiple indeterminacies in structure, will, and our knowledge, the simpler the structures, the more predictable the results. (Hence the popular acronym KISS: Keep It Simple, Stupid!) Accordingly, we seek to reduce problems to simpler terms. This works (witness modern science). It also leads to reducing ourselves, the line about "better a human being dissatisfied than a pig satisfied" notwithstanding.

The second problem is that power in itself, like structure and will, is incapable of supplying meaning. Our options thus are reduced to declaring the world meaningless or integrating ourselves into some higher-level system, either for the sake of God or for the sake of power.

But *how* do higher-level systems provide meaning? To answer that question, Shuster proposes the following model for power that builds on the previous discussion of structure and will by adding the column on the left:

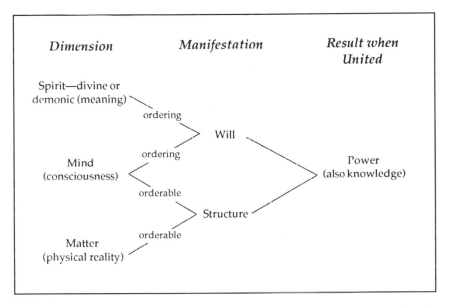

The left-hand column posits three dimensions: spirit, mind, and matter. First, mind and matter. "Matter is to mind as a line is to a plane —included in it, necessary to its expression, but wholly inadequate to produce it" (1987, 103). Mind fills matter to the degree that the particular form of matter allows it. Rocks, plants, animals, humans form a continuum. Given this continuum, the interesting question is not why psychokinesis occurs, but why it doesn't occur more often.

Second, the dimension of the spirit. The spiritual dimension contains both good and evil, either of which can supply meaning. The spiritual dimension encompasses not only God, but also other spirits, as well as anything which is made a source of ultimate meaning.

> Like consciousness with respect to matter, the spiritual is
> as fully present as it can be in both mind and matter but

> is in no way derivable from them. Will [in the middle
> column of the figure] is anchored from below in con-
> sciousness, without which it is impossible, and sus-
> pended from above by meaning, without which it would
> have nothing to do. In other words, when will purposes
> or chooses, it always draws its energy (or possibility for
> action) from the spiritual dimension (1987, 103).

As in Kelsey's model, we are always relating to the spiritual realm.
Meaning comes from outside ourselves. And this model fits, Shuster
argues, with New Testament anthropology. Whether God's spirit ordering the human will, or the "spirit of the world" ordering it, we are always
connected.

What are the implications for mission here?

First, the model reveals our daily contact with the spiritual. Our
wills, our reasons for doing this or that, are always drawing on the
spiritual. To be independent of this realm would be to be comatose.

Second, in so doing, it suggests multiple relationships with various
occupants of the spiritual realm, and hence a way of thinking about how
we are related individually to the powers. (This is not a question of
"possession," but simply of what it means to participate in multiple
structures.) On this point, however, there is at least a difference in emphasis with Kelsey. Kelsey pursues the question of how one relates positively
to each of the archetypes under the sovereignty of the Risen Christ.
Shuster focuses on the issue of whether the Risen Christ or someone/thing
else is exercising sovereignty.

Third, it emphasizes the profound importance of the choices people make. Mind-body research, physics, and Christian tradition together
highlight the reality-defining character of choice. It is not—to oversim-
plify—that Satan, the powers, people, and so on are fighting over the same
world, but that each person is creating and choosing different worlds.

> "There is no metaphysical system that "correctly" de-
> scribes reality. Each valid system . . . includes different
> "basic limiting principles," different definitions of what
> is "normal" and what is "paranormal" within them. . . .
> The metaphysical system you are using is the metaphys-
> ical system that is operating" (LeShan, cited in Shuster
> 1987, 62).

Berkhof, it will be remembered, argued that the power which the principalities and powers exercise is not primarily physical, but ideological, in
their claims to legitimacy and power. To engage the powers is thus to
argue about which claims correspond to (unchanging) reality. Shuster

offers a more radical way of seeing this engagement: the claims in question really create, and do not simply define, our reality. In *This Present Darkness*, Professor Langstrat, Pastor Busche, and the spirits Rafar and Tal are all operating in a common reality; Shuster's model suggests the possibility of a rather different novel.

Fourth, the model emphasizes the importance of the church in mission. Jesus speaks of the church not being of the world, but sent into the world (John 17:16, 18). Paul speaks of the church as an interconnected body (1 Cor. 12:12, 26-27). "What," asks Shuster, "if such assertions were not mere metaphors but sober fact" (1987, 63)?

> To press the example further, remember that, since we conceive will or choice to be a factor in what systems are operating, the possibility of one system capitulating to another or being impinged upon by it is always present. Hence the continual warnings to God's people that they are not to love the world, and also the initial physical separation of the Jews from the surrounding culture that would undermine their faith. However, events ostensibly determined by one field can also be incorporated constructively in (or, better, can also be determined by) another, as in the case of Joseph's brothers: what they meant for evil, God meant—and used—for good (Gen. 50:20). But if Joseph had been operating in a simply worldly way, he could have failed to see God's hand at work and have proceeded to execute his brothers. He had to choose which field defined what had happened and then make the appropriate response.
>
> The visible church has only clues badly followed as to what it would mean to be the true church. Fields, like paradigms, entail indwelling and commitment. There are conditions—any field we choose as determinative of our lives imposes conditions. "No one can serve two masters" (Matt. 6:24) (1987, 63).

In sum, Shuster's approach shows how we are inter-related to the spiritual dimension in any non-trivial decision and exercise of power. It provides a way of picturing our relationship to the powers. It underlines the significance of human choice. Finally, it underlines the importance of the church as a place of indwelling and commitment, as, to use Lohfink's phrase, a contrast-society.

Summary

1. To what texts does this
   tradition characteristically
   appeal?

   No particular group of text is characteristic.

2. Are the powers personal
   spiritual beings?

   Kelsey's Jungian interpretation would yield a negative response. Hiebert tends to follow Wink at this point (1990). Shuster would see the powers as personal spiritual beings.

How do we distinguish between appearance and reality? All the authors here would see this as a fundamental question. And all would agree that there is always an important difference between our varied understandings of reality and Reality. So far we are on familiar philosophical turf. Hiebert's contribution is to remind us that these various constructions of reality are also culturally and socially determined. So part of buying into Jung or Whitehead ought to be to understand why this decision makes sense within one's own life setting. Shuster's contribution is to point out that to some degree our choices determine the reality within which we operate.

3. Are the powers integrally
   connected to cultures,
   societies, etc.?

   Yes.

4. Are the powers more or less
   independent beings?

   Neither Kelsey nor Hiebert see the powers as part of a hierarchy. Shuster's work on will, structure, and power tends to neutralize this contrast: it does not seem possible to be an "independent."

5. Where is the activity of the
   powers a missiological
   concern?

   Hiebert's work has moved from a rural to an urban focus. Kelsey and Shuster's work has been centered in counseling.

6. What is the paradigmatic
   form of spiritual warfare?

   There is no one paradigmatic form.

7. Are the powers engaged directly in spiritual warfare?

    Both Kelsey's and Shuster's models suggest various ways in the which the powers are related directly on the personal level.

8. Does spiritual warfare mean using a qualitatively different sort of power than our foes?

    Yes, in the case of Hiebert. Kelsey and Shuster do not address the question.

9. Does spiritual warfare involve seeking to save the powers?

    Yes, conclude Hiebert and Kelsey, although using different models. Shuster does not address the question.

10. Does spiritual warfare call us into question in any fundamental way?

    Yes. Kelsey and Shuster see us as inevitably having some relationship to the powers. In Hiebert's model, we are continually called into question as we are tempted to play by satanic rules: to crush, rather than to heal.

SIX

Reaching for a Consensus:
Summary

IN *PILGRIM'S REGRESS*, C. S. Lewis suggested that major cultural shifts, such as Europe's discovery of chivalry, were one of the ways God used to keep us searching for his kingdom. This may be part of what is going on as our beliefs in rationality, enlightenment science, human autonomy and management by objective are being shaken and remolded.

Christians concerned for mission and living in the midst of these upheavals are returning to what Scripture has to say about the principalities and powers. They are doing so within various traditions. We have summarized how the Reformed, Anabaptist, third wave, and social science traditions have struggled to understand the role of the principalities and powers in mission. In this chapter we will summarize where these groups agree and disagree. We will then suggest some issues for dialogue between them.

To review, we have used *Reformed, Anabaptist, third wave,* and *social science* as broad types (with the last overlapping the first three):

The Reformed tradition	emphasizes transforming the power mediated by social structures toward greater compatibility with the gospel
The Anabaptist tradition	emphasizes the freedom given by the gospel over against the power mediated by social structures
The third wave tradition	emphasizes miraculous divine power in contrast to the

	power mediated by social structures
The social science tradition	attempts to relate the biblical language about the powers to models of reality developed by using the social sciences

"Reformed" and "Anabaptist" are used as a short-hand for the contrast between understanding the gospel as transforming the powers, over against seeing the gospel as an alternative to the powers. While the contrast reflects historic divisions within Protestantism, it is used more broadly here, cutting across the Protestant/Catholic divide. "Third wave" was coined by C. Peter Wagner, and points to a set of evangelical attempts to appropriate the power of the Spirit in highly visible ways in a variety of ministries. The fourth category, social science, is a different sort of grouping, whose representatives could also be placed in the first three groups. What holds this grouping together is the attempt to relate the biblical language about the principalities and powers to models of reality developed by using the social sciences.

Most people in the traditions surveyed would agree on the points which follow. All of these points have important implications for mission.

1. Scripture's references to the principalities and powers denote something real today. They are not leftover language of a more primitive era. Therefore, understanding the principalities and powers is relevant to how we plan and implement mission today. A number of mission challenges cannot be met apart from understanding the role of and responding to the powers.

2. Concern for the person means concern for the person's environment, and a person's environment is affected in major ways by the principalities and powers. This underscores the danger in creating a dichotomy between individuals and the communities in which they live. Thus Raymond Fung spelled out the meaning of the person as sinner and sinned against by pointing to the powers:

   We would like to report to the churches that man is lost, lost not only in the sins in his own heart but also in the sinning grasp of principalities and powers of the world, demonic forces which cast a bondage over human lives and human institutions and infiltrate their very textures (CWME 1980, 85).

3. While there is a difference between demonic activity as it affects institutions or individuals, the border is often fuzzy. This statement does not equate the powers with demons, but does take advantage of the various ways in which the word "demonic" is used. In any case, strategies for mission and pastoral care with regard to the demonic will increasingly overlap.

4. The church when it is truly the church is the most telling challenge to the powers. This is one of the central claims of the Anabaptist tradition, and is present also in Berkhof. Dawson and White appear to support this view as well. Thus programs for church renewal and programs for community renewal might be linked together. And this linkage might sharpen the focus of both.

5. The powers can be given too much attention. This is implicit among the Reformed and Anabaptists, as they generally mention the powers while talking about something else (usually social ethics). It is also present in the third wave as folk like White work to sketch a broader context in which spiritual warfare occurs. Thus mission strategies with weak theological moorings may be swept out to sea by an overemphasis on spiritual warfare.

These points of agreement are important, for they point to a dimension which we may increasingly need to incorporate into our mission efforts. Further, they point to a common process of discovery within which differences can be worked through.

Turning to the questions we have been asking, what answers have the different traditions given? Again, we are using very broad brush strokes here. As a result, the distance between traditions may be overstated, and differences within traditions understated. Where there is a significant 'minority report,' it is given in parentheses. For instance, in question two, while most in the Reformed tradition answer "no," some answer "yes," and thus we list "No (Yes)." Where a question is not addressed by a tradition, we indicate this with "Not addressed."

1. To what texts does this tradition characteristically appeal?

Reformed	Col. 1:13-15, 19
Anabaptist	Isa. 2:2-4; Mark 10:42-45

| Third Wave | Matt. 12:29; Eph. 6:12 |
| Social Science | Not addressed |

This listing highlights the differences between traditions. As frequently happens, the tradition is strongly influencing which texts are perceived as relevant. At the same time, texts such as Eph. 3:10 or 6:12 are cited by people from different traditions.

2. Are the powers personal spiritual beings?

Reformed	No (Yes)
Anabaptist	No (Yes)
Third Wave	Yes
Social Science	No (Yes)

Only the third wave group gives a uniform answer; the others give mixed responses. The biblical texts can be read in different ways. But the issue is deeper than whether or not the powers are personal. The fundamental questions are how we understand the New Testament's language today —and how we understand our world.

Appeals to simply "believe the Bible" are not very helpful here. For example, Genesis 1 speaks both of a solid firmament which keeps the rainwater in place and in which the stars are placed and of the beasts of the field. Our pictures of the world contain the beasts of the field, but include the firmament only with major adjustments. Are the principalities and powers more like the firmament, or the beasts of the field? There is hard theological work to be done on this area.

3. Are the powers integrally connected to cultures, societies, etc?

Reformed	Yes
Anabaptist	Yes
Third Wave	No (Yes)
Social Science	Yes

The Reformed see the powers as integral to institutions and other phenomena. This is at the heart of their discovery that the New Testament's talk about the powers matches our experience with institutions. The powers are thus inseparable from the institutions. The Anabaptist and social science groups generally agree with this view.

The third wavers see the powers more as high-level demons who work through or infest institutions. That is, they see the powers as separable from institutions and cultures. Therefore they can talk about binding or exorcising the powers.

The Reformed see the powers as bringing both order and disorder; the third wave see them as only bringing disorder. Thus when the Reformed hear the third wave group discuss the possibility of exorcising the spirit presiding over Chicago, they may wonder if going through O'Hare Airport is not already challenging enough!

While the Reformed tradition appears to do justice to more of the texts in Scripture here, neither position is without difficulties. The Reformed tradition appears to underplay the fundamentally rebellious character of the powers (as the Anabaptist tradition regularly points out). The third wave tradition too quickly combines the powers and the demons. For instance, Jesus cast demons out of people, but wept over Jerusalem. Could Jesus have bound the territorial spirits of Chorazin, Bethsaida, Capernaum, and Jerusalem? Again, Jesus dealt with both demoniacs and Herodians, but the latter group had more to do with putting him on the Cross. The serious opposition to the gospel came from groups to which exorcism was not a response.

The problem is to find language that will help us plan and do different sorts of mission. The Reformed model speaks to the task of living with the powers. Can one really be Japanese and Christian? A Yankee and a Christian? Where the missiological issue is contextualization, Reformed models may be of more use. The third wave model speaks to the task of freeing ourselves from the forces of death (powers? demons?). Where the missiological issue is syncretism, we may want to draw on third wave models. The tasks are clearly not mutually exclusive, but we will need to take care not to work at cross-purposes.

4.   Are the powers more or less independent agents?

Reformed	Yes
Anabaptist	Yes
Third Wave	No
Social Science	Not addressed (No)

The third wave option believes that the principalities and powers are part of a satanic hierarchy. The other traditions tend to see the powers as more or less independent, or, better, as interrelated in the same ways that our institutions are interrelated. Shuster's work on will, structure, and power tends to neutralize this contrast: being an "independent" does not appear to be an option.

The consequences for mission cluster around the question of what expectations we bring with us as we deal with structures. How hard do we work not to pre-judge what the response of one of the powers will be in any given circumstance? Will we find an open door or a closed door when we go down to City Hall? We don't know, but as Eller's description of his son's trial suggests, a refusal to (further) polarize a situation may serve as an invitation for God's grace to operate.

5.   Where is the activity of the powers a missiological concern?

Reformed	Where there is injustice in society
Anabaptist	Hierarchial structures in society or church
Third Wave	Where evangelism is blocked
Social Science	Not addressed

The different responses raise a number of questions: To what degree do the differences reflect different worldviews or different callings? Could we work towards a worldview within which the different vocations could all be celebrated?

Further work is also needed with regard to which set of mission issues the various traditions identify as most important. The third wave critical issue list tends to be conservative politically and theologically. Other lists are predictably "left-wing." None of us have made much progress in escaping from our own cultural captivity, for we rarely notice our chains.

Put another way, while we wish to avoid being demonized by something smelling of sulfur, do we not enjoy being demonized by GE ("We bring good things to life") and Nissan ("Designed for the human race")?

6.   What is the paradigmatic form of spiritual warfare?

Reformed	Social action
Anabaptist	Church as contrast-society
Third Wave	Evangelism
Social Science	Not addressed

The answers given to this question largely follow from how each tradition understands the activities of the powers (see previous question). At the same time, all the traditions stress resources such as prayer at this point (although it is interesting to note that none give much attention to the role of the sacraments). An encouraging sign is the number of ministry models which combine a variety of approaches, whether Mott's *Biblical Ethics and Social Change* or White's *The Believer's Guide to Spiritual Warfare*. The greatest danger here appears to be the marginalization of the vision of the church as contrast-society in mission discussions. Yet Berkhof saw the issue of the quality of church life as central. This may reflect some avoidance. It is easier and less painful to plan to change others.

7. Are the powers engaged directly in spiritual warfare?

Reformed	No (Yes)
Anabaptist	No
Third Wave	Yes
Social Science	Not addressed

This question is tied to the third question. Where the powers are seen as integrally related to institutions, they are generally engaged as institutions are engaged. Where the powers are seen as separate, they are generally engaged directly through exorcism.

On the other hand, Wink suggests we should understand social protest as a form of exorcism. But what does he expect will happen? The third wavers expect the spirits to leave—or at least be checked. Could Omar Cabrera and Walter Wink engage in a joint action?

Put differently, we have two sorts of missiological questions here. First, while Bill Kellermann sees the angel of Detroit as a potential ally, the third wavers tend to see the angel of Detroit as a candidate for exorcism. This appears to be a clear-cut choice, but it would be worth exploring a bit further before casting our ballots. Second, whatever answer we give, how does dealing with the powers get integrated into the rest of our activities?

8. Does spiritual warfare mean using a qualitatively different sort of power than our foes?

Reformed	No (Yes)
Anabaptist	Yes
Third Wave	No
Social Science	Not addressed (No)

The extremes on this question would be Hiebert's analysis of the different models of warfare, which stresses the difference between the sorts of power used, and Peretti's battles. But "qualitatively different sort of power" needs sorting out. How do power and weakness interrelate in spiritual warfare? In what senses is Christian spiritual warfare cruciform?

The missiological questions here are important, but not always obvious. Here are three examples. First, how does our faith influence the ways we use power within Christian institutions? Second, when we attempt to persuade, whether we label the setting "evangelistic" or "social policy," what limits does our faith place on the sorts of techniques of persuasion we employ? Third, what counts as success? The ways we answer questions such as these will make it more or less likely that some modern Hosea will rightly tell us that though we say we are following Yahweh, we are still serving Baal.

9. Does spiritual warfare involve seeking to save the powers?

Reformed	Yes
Anabaptist	No (Yes)
Third Wave	No
Social Science	Not addressed

Again, the responses to this question flow from the responses to question three. One way of putting the question is to recall John's vision of the New Jerusalem:

By its light shall the nations walk; and the kings of the
earth shall bring their glory into it, and its gates shall
never be shut by day—and there shall be no night there;
they shall bring into it the glory and the honor of the
nations (Rev. 21:4-6).

Are the principalities and powers here too? If so, what would it mean to
evangelize the powers? How do you evangelize an institution? How do
you call it back to its true vocation?

10. Does spiritual warfare call us into question in any fundamental way?

Reformed	Yes
Anabaptist	Yes
Third Wave	No (Yes)
Social Science	Not addressed

Anthropologists have long noted that accusations of witchcraft
play a predictable role when societies are in crisis. Whether these accusations contribute anything useful to the society's knowledge of spiritual
warfare or not, they provide to the anthropologist clear clues regarding
the society's pathologies. Demonizing one's opponent is one of the oldest
debating tricks around. What these two somewhat crude examples suggest is that, unless our language about spiritual warfare forces us to
confront ourselves more honestly, then it is a virtual certainty that we are
simply using it as a way of reinforcing positions we hold for other reasons.
This means we are losing spiritual battles of which we are not even aware.
By the grace of God, examples of spiritual warfare which are healthy from
this perspective are present in all the traditions surveyed.

We may summarize these varied responses as follows:

Reformed	*Anabaptist*	*Third Wave*	*Social Science*
1. To what texts does this tradition characteristically appeal?			
Col 1:13-15,19	Isa 2:2-4; Mk 10:42-45	Mt 12:29; Eph 6:12	Not addressed
2. Are the powers personal spiritual beings?			
No (Yes)	No (Yes)	Yes	No (Yes)
3. Are the powers integrally connected to cultures, societies, etc?			
Yes	Yes	No (Yes)	Yes

Reformed	Anabaptist	Third Wave	Social Science
4. Are the powers more or less independent agents?			
Yes	Yes	No	Not addressed (No)
5. Where is the activity of the powers a missiological concern?			
Where there is injustice in society	Hierarchial structures in society or church	Where evangelism is blocked	Not addressed
6. What is the paradigmatic form of spiritual warfare?			
Social action	Church as contrast society	Evangelism	Not addressed
7. Are the powers engaged directly in spiritual warfare?			
No (Yes)	No	Yes	Not addressed
8. Does spiritual warfare mean using a qualitatively different sort of power than our foes?			
No (Yes)	Yes	No	Not addressed
9. Does spiritual warfare involve seeking to save the powers?			
Yes	No (Yes)	No	Not addressed
10. Does spiritual warfare call us into question in any fundamental way?			
Yes	Yes	No (Yes)	Not addressed

What kinds of conversations between traditions might be useful?

A Reformed-Anabaptist conversation has been under way for some time. The issue most interesting for our discussion is how Christians relate to the power mediated by institutions. The question involves at least one's understanding of creation, Jesus, the kingdom and the church. Yoder's *The Politics of Jesus* and Mott's *Biblical Ethics and Social Change* are particularly key contributions to this conversation. Oddly, while both use the language of the principalities and powers, neither appears to get much mileage out of it. Perhaps this is because the Bible gives us too little information on the powers, or because our picture of the powers simply reflects our decisions on more fundamental matters (creation, Christology, and so on). Perhaps there's something here worth exploring further.

The Reformed conversation with the third wave tradition has yet to happen in a publically useful way. The Reformed questions to the third wave might include: Are you ignoring the multiple ways in which we may be seduced by the powers? How would you address the danger of promoting a private faith which leaves the fundamental power relationships within a society unchallenged? Some repressive regimes are only too willing to welcome some evangelists. While abortion clinics, pornography shops, or New Age bookstores might not be bad places to start, does limiting one's attention to these adequately address the hold the powers have on our cities?

These questions relate to the often ahistorical nature of the third wave position. What would their analysis look like if the historical dimension were taken more seriously? In the case of South Korea, part of the appeal of the church is surely due to the church's sharing Korean nationalist aspirations during the Japanese occupation. A broader view of the powers could lead to a broader set of questions being asked—even in evangelism.

On the other hand, the third wave questions to the Reformed might go something like this: Do you pray enough, fast enough, have enough expectancy about what God might do quite apart from your doubtless competent analyses? Do you really believe in the efficacy of God's sovereign power in mission? In your focus on social and psychological analyses, have you adequately accounted for the supernatural dimensions of the war between the kingdom of God and the kingdom of this world? Are you and your missiology still too captive to an enlightenment, scientific worldview? What is an adequate mission response to animist beliefs in shamans, territorial spirits, magic and curses and actual field experience with tangible expressions of power on the part of these?

The conversation between the social sciences and the other traditions is taking place in the persons of those who are working at integration (for instance, Shuster, Hiebert, Kraft from the Reformed, Anabaptist, and third wave traditions respectively). The questions being asked include: What account of the world do we use? (What decisions about what sorts of powers are operative in the world do we need to make?) Initial studies like Berkhof's worked within the Biblical Theology movement, in which the Bible's world was taken to be our world. Hence Berkhof is not overly concerned with the precise ontological contours of the powers. Wink's focus is not ontology, but his heavy use of Jung and Whitehead raises the ontological question. Hiebert raises the ontological issue both as anthropologist and missionary. Once one starts working with multiple societies with conflicting worldviews, one can't simply accept each group's worldview. One has to make reality decisions which may differ from one's society. And this is an issue for understanding the New Testament as well.

None of these conversations will be easy. The hardest part about writing this monograph was keeping my own preferences in check. Some readers may doubt that I succeeded. Nevertheless, they are conversations we need, and may this piece be an encouragement to them.

One last point. The focus of this study has been on the principalities and powers relevant to mission "out there." We identified the Reformed, Anabaptist, third wave, and social science types or traditions as ways of approaching this issue. Are these not also powers themselves? We might also need to concern ourselves with the powers of different theological traditions. Borrowing a page from Berkhof, these powers both facilitate our faith and practice and erect barriers, whether characteristic blind spots or the multiple difficulties in cooperating with those of different orientations.

What does this mean? There would be more than a little irony in our being hampered in our struggle against the powers "out there" by taking insufficient account of the strengths and weaknesses of the powers "in here" (our very theological traditions themselves).

Therefore, our work to understand, learn from, and cooperate with each other, far from being a distraction, may be at the center of dealing with the powers.

> For we are not contending against flesh and blood, but
> against the principalities, against the powers . . .

The New Testament Word Field for "Powers"

WHAT WORDS are used for the powers? The following list of words and texts represents an initial cut. The list of words follows Louw & Nida (#12.44), whose recent lexicon lists words by semantic domain or field (like a thesaurus).[1]

The English word following is the word generally used in the *New Revised Standard Version*. The list of occurrences is cross-checked against both Bauer-Arndt-Gingrich and Kittel lexicons. In most cases the words have other meanings as well, so not all the texts in which the words occur are cited. This list should be compared with the rather fuller listings in Kelsey (1978, 146-49).

Words & texts

aion	"age"	Eph. 2:2; 3:9; Col. 1:26. So BAG (27 #4, with bibliography). Sasse regards Eph. 2:2 as possible; rejects Eph. 2:7; 3:9; Col. 1:26 (*TDNT* 1:197-209).

---

1   Lexical references cited:

BAG   Bauer, Walter, William F. Arndt, & F. Wilbur Gingrich. 1957. *A Greek-English Lexicon of the New Testament and other early Christian literature*. Chicago: Univ. of Chicago Pr.; Cambridge: Cambridge U P.

LN   Louw, Johannes P. & Eugene A. Nida, eds. 1988. *Greek-English Lexicon of the New Testament based on semantic domains*. 2 vols. New York. United Bible Societies.

MG   Mouton & Gedden. *A Greek Concordance to the New Testament*.

TDNT   Kittel, Gerhard, ed. 1964-76. *Theological Dictionary of the New Testament*. 10 vols. Grand Rapids: Eerdmans.

arche	"ruler"	Luke 12:11*; 20:20*; Rom. 8:38; 1 Cor. 15:24; Eph. 1:21; 3:10; 6:12; Col. 1:16; 2:10,15; Titus 3:1*; Jude 6** (* = human referent; ** = "rule"). So BAG (111-12 #3,4). Delling notes regular collocation with *exousia*, with exception of Jude 6 (*TDNT* 1:478-89). Appears 56x in NT (MG 110-111).
archon	"ruler"	Matt. 9:34; 12:24; Mark 3:22; Luke 11:15; John 12:31; 14:30; 16:11 (refers to devil); 1 Cor. 2:6-8; Eph. 2:2. So BAG (113 #3), Delling (*TDNT* 1:478-89).
dunamis	"power"	Matt. 24:29//Mark 13:25//Luke 21:26; Rom. 8:38; 1 Cor. 15:24; Eph. 1:21; 1 Peter 3:22. So BAG (206-207 #6, citing also Acts 8:10; omitting Matt. 24:29par), Grundmann (*TDNT* 2:284-317).
exousia	"authority"	Luke 12:11*; Rom 13:1[bis]*,2*,3*; 1 Cor. 15:24; Eph. 1:21; 3:10; 6:12; Col. 1:16; 2:10,15; Titus 3:1*; 1 Peter 3:22 (* = human referent). So BAG (277-28, #4c, with bibliography, and including Eph. 2:2 "domain of the air"). See Foerster for general discussion and bibliography (*TDNT* 2:560-575). Appears 102x in NT (MG 347-48).
thronos	"throne"	Col. 1:16. So BAG (364-65 #2b), Schmitz (*TDNT* 3:160-167).
kosmokrator	"cosmic power"	Eph. 6:12. So BAG (446), Michaelis (*TDNT* 3:905-15).
kuriotes	"dominion"	Eph. 1:21; Col. 1:16. So BAG (461-62 #3), Foerster (*TDNT* 3:1096-97). Appears 4x in NT.

pneumatikon	"spiritual force"	Eph. 6:12. So BAG (685 #3).

Texts & words

The following table gives a cross-section of the occurence of the words for "powers" in The New Testament.

Below the table is an explanation of the abbreviated headings.

	are	*aro*	*du*	*ex*	*ai*	*th*	*ko*	*ku*	*pn*
Matt. 24:29			*						
Mark 13:25			*						
Luke 12:11	*			*					
Luke 20:20	*								
Luke 21:26			*						
Rom. 8:38	*		*						
Rom. 13:1-3				*					
1 Cor. 2:6, 8		*							
1 Cor. 15:24	*		*	*					
Eph. 1:21	*		*					*	
Eph. 2:2		*			*				
Eph. 3:9					*				
Eph. 3:10	*			*					
Eph. 6:12	*			*			*		*
Col. 1:16	*			*		*		*	
Col. 1:26					*				
Col. 2:10	*			*					
Col. 2:15	*			*					
Titus 3:1	*			*					
1 Peter 3:22			*	*					
Jude 6		*							

are	=	arche "ruler"	*th*	=	thronos "throne"
aro	=	archon "ruler"	*ko*	=	kosmotrator "cosmic power"
du	=	dunamis "power"	*ku*	=	kuriotes "dominion"
ex	=	exousia "authority"	*pn*	=	pneumatikon "spiritual force"
ai	=	aion "age"			

Mission Model: The "Plan Resistencia"

THE "PLAN RESISTENCIA" is a unique church-planting, evangelistic strategy designed to evangelize an entire city. It counts baptisms and new churches rather than just decision cards. It aims at literally reaching every house with the gospel. Working together with Harvest Evangelism, local pastors of this city of 400,000 want to grow from their existing 6,000 combined membership (1.5% of the population) to 48,000 (12%) in the next three years. And that would only be the beginning. Because of its strategic location, Resistencia holds the keys to unlocking Argentina's seven northern provinces to hearing the good news of Jesus Christ.

The first stop of the plan calls for dividing the entire city into 500 squares, each one containing approximately 800 people. A Christian individual, couple or family will be assigned to each square. Over the next 12 months these Christians will open a house-church (a "lighthouse") in each of the 500 locations. They will visit the shut-ins, pray for the sick, feed the hungry, and minister to the poor. The main objective is to "gain favor in the eyes of the people," as was the case in the book of Acts (Acts 2:47).

In July 1990, the evangelistic phase begins with an ever-increasing scope and depth. First, there will be house-to-house visitations of the entire city climaxed with 50 simultaneous week-long crusades led by local evangelists. The following week more experienced evangelists will lead 10 simultaneous one-week crusades using larger auditoriums. And finally, everybody will go to the largest city soccer stadium for the final week of proclaiming the gospel. During this week the region will be saturated with mass media, using radio, TV, and newspapers, as well as ladies' teas and businessmen's luncheons to aggressively preach the gospel to every creature in Resistencia.

But this is not all. The week after the major outreach the church plans to go back to the 10 locations where the crusades were held. This time the evangelists and the pastors, working hand-in-hand, will teach the Bible to the new converts for five evenings, Monday through Friday. And then Saturday will be "D" day....

Saturday, beginning at 10:00 a.m. at the soccer stadium, local pastors will baptize new converts. Probably thousands of them! Can you imagine the joy in heaven as scores of new babes in Christ give public testimony of their faith in Christ our Lord? The following day, Sunday, the church will return to the stadium and even though the gospel will be preached again, the main focus will be celebration of the Lord's Supper. As many as 40,000 believers could gather together to proclaim the Lordship of Christ over Resistencia!

Then on Monday, everybody goes back to their lighthouses, which by then should be operating as full-fledged congregations. There could be as many as 500 of these!

Seven Distinctives of the "Plan Resistencia"

1. The rediscovery of the principle of gaining favor in the eyes of the people by ministering to their needs regardless of their response to the gospel message.

2. The entire body of Christ working together, as one body, with no excessive denominational emphasis. This is possible due to the tremendous level of unity existing among many pastors in Resistencia.

3. The thorough penetration of the city 12 months prior to the outreach. The "filling up of Jerusalem with our doctrine" can only be done by doing it house to house.

4. Presentation of a gospel message that is complete so as to enable the new believers to be baptized as soon as they receive the Word as was the pattern in the book of Acts. This approach calls for the evangelist to present a gospel message that places the local church at the heart of it.

5. By establishing the planning of new churches and the number of baptisms as the standard of measure, rather than the number of decision cards, the Plan Resistencia offers a more Biblical alternative to the old fashioned and ineffective approach of counting cards. Local churches are living organisms. Once established they remain established. A local church has been gifted by God with the elements of survival. On the other hand, an isolated believer does not have that advantage.

6. By leading the new believers to be baptized immediately, they will engage in proclaiming to the powers that used to

rule them that ownership has been transferred; that Jesus Christ is their master and "no one is able to snatch them out of the Father's hand." It is expected that a very large number of those baptized will remain in the church as a result of this approach.

7. Finally, by establishing hundreds of new congregations, even if they are small house-churches, a footing will be provided to stand firm after having done everything, as it is said in Eph. 6:14.

Mission Model: Discerning the "Angel" of a City

THE CONGRESS BIBLE STUDY may serve as the basis for a "discernment group" in any city. Following are some suggestions for ways to expand the process.

1. It is best that the group be made up of people engaged in ministry or social struggle within the city. This is not a disinterested academic exercise.

2. Commit for a specific period of time (6-10 weeks, say).

3. Share what "spiritual disciplines" people regularly employ (prayer, meditation, journal-keeping, Scripture study, poetry writing, common worship). Will everyone commit to bringing the city as an entity into those disciplines for the duration of the group? Each group meeting ought to include some form of common prayer or contemplation and some Bible study.

4. Common readings from Walter Wink *(Naming the Powers)* may be of help for further background. Or the review essay on his work in *Sojourners*, May 1987.

5. An exercise: collectively reconstruct from memory the history of your city. Create a time line. Be especially conscious of crossroads, turning points, decisive events, larger historical forces. From whose perspective has the story been told? How have elements of your city's history become its "myth," the story which popularly conveys its identity?

6. Perhaps there is an article-length social history of your city available or a social analysis of where the city is at the present moment. This may be best read after the reconstruction.

7. Because the task is to listen and see with new sensitivity, a session with an urban poet may be fruitful. She/he might do a reading for the group, but also talk about the personal process of poetry writing.

8. List signs of death in the city. Signs of hope and life.

9. Another exercise: list places that people would stand to discern the "voice of the city" or to see the face of "the angel of the city." Perhaps one or more of the groups' sessions could actually meet in such places.

10. One person to lead others in guided meditation (modeled on Dan. 10 and Rev. 1-2): breathing and relaxation; go to the "place" where you would listen/look for "angel of the city;" take in sounds, smells, any people present, turn to see One like a Human Being ("the Son of Man"); fall on your face as though dead (To what do I need to die in order to hear the Word?); rise and listen to the word for your city ("say to the Angel of _____"); turn again—where are you? same place? changed? how? take it in; now turn to see the angel of the city—feelings/color? shape? human form?; ask, "Who are you? and "What are you saying in this moment?;" convey the Word from the Human One; return to your place.

11. Without speaking, take up paper and pens and begin to draw images out of your meditation. Or: take up clay and begin to work it; think with your hands; form the "angel;" this needn't be artistic or creative; share the results in group conversation.

12. A writing exercise to be done individually:

Choose one of these three possible formats for the listening/writing project: a) The Voice of the City; what is it saying to you about itself in this historical moment? b) The Word of God as addressed to the city in this particular moment: ("To the Angel of _____, write this...") c) A dialogue using both of the above or yourself as interlocutor.

- Where will you stand to listen? (You may in reality want to situate yourself in a particular environs, geography, social location.)
- Prepare yourself for listening. Identify and acknowledge your own self-interests, class interests, and institutional self-interests with respect to the city. How do these block your vision/hearing?
- Read Rev. 1:1-2:7. What is the relationship between the angels of the church and the One like a Human Being? Using the analogy, hold your city before the clear presence of the Human One (Son of Man). What does he say to the angel of your city?
- Or reread Luke 13:34-35; 19:41-44. Replace "Jerusalem" with the name of your city. Does it ring true in any way or strike a chord in you? If it is a help, imagine Christ entering the city (at what point?). What else does he say?

- What do you love about your city? Actually make a list of things. Are they primarily visible or "invisible" aspects of the city? Do the visible and invisible aspects reflect one another?

- Where is the city in bondage to death? to forces and powers (economic, political, spiritual) greater which use and abuse it? In what ways does the city place its own "survival" above the life of its citizens? What would it look like to be liberated from these bondages?

- Choose one of the three formats and begin to write. Write freely, uncritically, unself-consciously. Now go back and edit. Bring it into form and shape.

13. Bring these "prophesies and voices," admittedly subjective, back to the group. Perhaps they might be shared in the context of a group liturgy. Together they represent a kind of collective discernment. They might also be used in other contexts, as a reading to begin a community meeting or such.

14. Concluding discussion: how do these readings of the city, its potentiality, its vocation, its identity in calling and fallenness alter ministries or participation in social struggle in this moment of your city's history?

Prepared for 1990 Congress on Urban Ministry by
Bill Kellermann, 1994 Clarkdale, Detroit, MI 48209

BIBLIOGRAPHY

Abijole, Bayo. 1988. "St Paul's Concept of Principalities and Powers in African Context." *Africa Theological Journal* 17/2: 118-129.

Arnold, Clinton E. 1987. "The 'Exorcism' of Ephesians 6:12 in Recent Research: A Critique of Wesley Carr's View of the Role of Evil Powers in First Century AD Belief." *Journal for the Study of the New Testament* 30: 71-87.

_____. 1989. *Ephesians, Power and Magic: The Concept of Power in Ephesians in Light of its Historical Setting.* Society for New Testament Studies Monograph Series 63. Cambridge: Cambridge University Press.

Bärsch, Claus E. 1988. "Antijudaismus, Apokalpytik und Satanologie: Die Religiösen Elemente des Nationalsozialistischen Antisemitismus." *Zeitschrift für Religions - und Geistesgeschichte* 40/2: 112-133.

Benoit, Pierre. 1983. "Pauline Angelology and Demonology: Reflexions on Designations of Heavenly Powers and on Origin of Angelic Evil According to Paul." *Religious Studies Bulletin* 3/1: 1-18.

Berkhof, Hendrikus. 1962 [1953]. *Christ and the Powers.* Scottsdale PA: Herald Press.

Cabezas de Krumm, Rita. 1989. "Areas of Satanic Influence." A paper presented at the Lausanne II in Manila Spiritual Warfare Track. Photocopy.

Caird, G. B. 1956. *Principalities and Powers: A Study in Pauline Theology.* Oxford: The Clarendon Press.

Carr, Wesley. 1981. *Angels and Principalities: The Background, Meaning, and Development of the Pauline Phrase Hai Archai Kai Hai Exousiai.* Society for New Testament Studies Monograph Series 42. Cambridge: Cambridge University Press.

Commission on World Mission and Evangelism, World Council of Churches. 1980. *Your Kingdom Come: Mission Perspectives: Report on the World Conference on Mission and Evangelism, Melbourne, Australia 12-25 May 1980.* Geneva: World Council of Churches.

Cullmann, Oscar. 1956. *The State in the New Testament.* New York: Scribners.

Dawson, John. 1989. *Taking Our Cities for God: How to Break Spiritual Strongholds.* Lake Mary FL: Creation House. A leader's guide and student workbook is also available.

Eller, Vernard, ed. 1980. *Thy Kingdom Come: A Blumhardt Reader.* Grand Rapids: Eerdmans.

Eller, Vernard. 1987. *Christian Anarchy: Jesus' Primacy Over the Powers.* Grand Rapids: Eerdmans.

Green, Michael. 1981. *I Believe in Satan's Downfall.* Grand Rapids: Eerdmans.

Hezham, Irving. 1972. "Theology, Exorcism, and the Amplification of Deviancy." *Evangelical Quarterly* 49: 111-16.

Hiebert, Paul G. 1982. "The Flaw of the Excluded Middle." *Missiology* 10/1: 35-47.

Hinkelammert, Franz J. 1986. *The Ideological Weapons of Death: A Theological Critique of Capitalism.* Maryknoll: Orbis.

Hollenbach, Paul W. 1981. "Jesus, Demoniacs, and Public Authorities: A Socio-historical study." *Journal of the American Academy of Religion* 49/4: 567-88.

Igenoza, Andrew Olu. 1986. "Christian Theology and the Belief in Evil Spirits: an African Perspective." *Scottish Bulletin of Evangelical Theology* 4: 39-48.

Kellermann, Bill. 1989. "Discerning the Angel of Detroit: A Parable for Our Time." *Sojourners* 18/9: 16-21.

_____. 1991. *Seasons of Faith and Conscience.* Maryknoll: Orbis.

Kelsey, Morton. 1976. *The Other Side of Silence: A Guide to Christian Meditation.* New York: Paulist.

_____. 1978. *Discernment: A Study in Ecstasy and Evil.* New York: Paulist.

_____. 1989. *Reaching: The Journey to Fulfillment.* San Francisco: Harper & Row.

Kraft, Charles H. 1989. *Christianity with Power: Your Worldview and Your Experience of the Supernatural.* Ann Arbor: Servant.

Lohfink, Gerhard. 1984. *Jesus and Community: The Social Dimension of Christian Faith.* Philadelphia: Fortress & New York: Paulist.

Lohfink, Norbert, S.J. 1987. *Option for the Poor: The Basic Principle of Liberation Theology in the Light of the Bible.* Berkeley: Bibal.

Miller, Calvin. 1990. "Looking for the Devil in All the Wrong Places" [Interview]. *Wittenburg Door* 109: 5-9.

Morrison, Clinton. 1960. *The Powers That Be: Earthly Rulers and Demonic Powers in Romans 13:1-7.* Naperville IL: Alec R. Allenson.

Mott, Stephen Charles. 1982. *Biblical Ethics and Social Change. New York:* Oxford University Press.

Mouw, Richard J. 1976. *Politics and the Biblical Drama.* Grand Rapids: Eerdmans. 85-116.

_____. 1990. "Giving the Devil His Due" [Excerpt from *Distorted Truth*]. *Wittenburg Door* 109: 13-17.

Murphy, George L. 1988. "Toward a Theology of Technological War." *Dialog* [Minnesota] 27: 48-54.

Obijole, O. O. 1986. "The Concept of Principalities and Powers in St. Paul's Gospel of Reconciliation in African Context." *African Journal of Biblical Studies* 1/2.

Padilla, C. René. 1976. "Spiritual Conflict." *The New Face of Evangelicalism: An International Symposium on the Lausanne Covenant,* ed. C. René Padilla, 205-221. Downers Grove: InterVarsity Press.

Pannell, William E. 1980. "Evangelism and Power." *International Review of Mission* 69: 49-55.

Peck, M. Scott. 1983. *People of the Lie: The Hope for Healing Human Evil.* New York: Simon & Schuster, Inc.

Peretti, Frank E. 1986. *This Present Darkness.* Westchester IL: Crossway Books.

_____. 1989. *Piercing the Darkness.* Westchester IL: Crossway Books.

_____. 1990. "The Technicolor Exorcisms of Frank Peretti" [Interview]. *Wittenburg Door* 109: 5-9.

Powell, Cyril H. 1963. *The Biblical Concept of Power.* London: Epworth Press.

Rumph, Jane. 1990. Report of the Post-Lausanne II Consultation on Cosmic-Level Spiritual Warfare (Lake Avenue Congregational Church, Pasadena, California, 2/12/90). Photocopy.

Schlier, Heinrich. 1961. *Principalities and Powers in the New Testament.* New York: Herder & Herder.

Shuster, Marguerite. 1987. *Power, Pathology, Paradox: The Dynamics of Evil and Good.* Grand Rapids: Zondervan.

Sider, Ronald J. 1980. Christ and Power. *International Review of Mission* 69: 8-20.

Silvoso, Edgardo. 1989. "Spiritual Warfare in Argentina and the 'Plan Resistencia'." A paper presented at the Lausanne II in Manila Spiritual Warfare Track. Photocopy.

Southard, Samuel, and Donna Southard. 1986. "Demonizing and Mental Illness; pt 3: Explanations and Treatment, Seoul." *Pastoral Psychology* 35: 132-151.

Sterk, Vernon J. 1989. "Territorial Spirits and Evangelization in Hostile Environments." Fuller Theological Seminary School of World Mission paper. Reprinted in Wagner 1990.

Stewart, J. S. 1951. "On a Neglected Emphasis in New Testament Theology." *Scottish Journal of Theology* 4: 292-301.

Stringfellow, William. 1973. *An Ethic for Christians and Other Aliens in a Strange Land.* Waco, Tex: Word Books.

van den Heuvel, Albert. 1966. *Those Rebellious Powers.* London: SCM Press.

Wagner, C. Peter. 1986. "The Key to Victory is Binding the 'Strong Man'." *Ministries Today* (Nov/Dec 1986), 84.

Wagner, C. Peter, ed. 1987. *Signs and Wonders Today.* New expanded edition. Altamonte Springs FL: Creation House.

Wagner, C. Peter 1988a. *How to Have a Healing Ministry Without Making Your Church Sick.* Ventura CA: Regal Books

_____. 1988b. "Territorial Spirits." A Paper presented at the Academic Symposium on Power Evangelism, Fuller Seminary, December 13-15, 1988. Photocopy.

_____. 1988c. *The Third Wave of the Holy Spirit.* Ann Arbor MI: Vine Books

_____. 1989. "Territorial Spirits and World Missions." *Evangelical Missions Quarterly* 25/3: 278-88.

Wagner, C. Peter, ed. 1990. *Territorial Spirits Reader.* Photocopy.

Wagner, C. Peter & F. Douglas Pennoyer, eds. 1990. *Wrestling with Dark Angels: Toward a Deeper Understanding of the Supernatural Forces in Spiritual Warfare.* Ventura, Ca: Regal Books.

Wallis, Jim. 1976. *Agenda for Biblical People.* New York: Harper. 63-77.

Warner, Timothy M. 1988. "Power Encounter in World Evangelization." Fuller Theological Seminary 1988 Church Growth Lectures. Audio tapes.

Westerman, Chuck. 1990. "Demons and Disney World and Angels in the Muck." *Wittenburg Door* 109: 29-31.

White, John. 1988. *When the Spirit Comes with Power.* Downers Grove: IVP.

White, Tom. 1989. "A Model for Discerning, Penetrating, and Overcoming Ruling Principalities and Powers." A paper presented at the Lausanne II in Manila Spiritual Warfare Track. Photocopy.

_____. 1990. *The Believer's Guide to Spiritual Warfare: Wising up to Satan's Influence in Your World.* Ann Arbor MI: Servant Publications.

White, Victor, O.P. 1961. *God and the Unconscious.* Cleveland: World Publishing Co.

Wink, Walter. 1978. "Unmasking the Powers: A Biblical View of Roman and American economies." *Sojourners* 10/78: 9-15.

_____. 1984. *Naming the Powers: The Language of Power in the New Testament.* Philadelphia: Fortress Press.

_____. 1986. *Unmasking the Powers: The Invisible Forces that Determine Human Existence.* Philadelphia: Fortress Press.

_____. 1987. *Violence and Nonviolence in South Africa: Jesus' Third Way.* Philadelphia: New Society Publishers.

_____. 1990a. "Unmasking the Powers That Be" [Interview]. *Wittenburg Door* 109: 13-17.

_____. 1990b. "Is there an Ethic of Violence?" *The Way* April 103-13.

_____. 1990c. "Prayer: History Belongs to the Intercessors." *Sojourners* October 10-14.

_____. 1990d. "God is the intercessor: Christians Give Words to the Spirit's Longings." *Sojourners* November 23-24.

Yoder, John Howard. 1972. *The Politics of Jesus.* Grand Rapids: Eerdmans.